Purpose, Provision and Power

Tracey Muponda

Onwards and Upwards Publishers

Berkeley House, 11 Nightingale Crescent, Leatherhead,
Surrey, KT24 6PD.
www.onwardsandupwards.org

ISBN: 978-1-907509-81-0
Typeface: Sabon LT
Graphic design: Leah-Maarit

Out of respect, and in keeping with the tradition of certain Bible translations, the author has chosen to capitalise the first letter of certain words that pertain to God and his authority, e.g. Word, Kingdom, He/His/Him.

About the Author

Tracey is married to Gwinyai and they have three children. She runs a number of businesses in the UK and internationally, and has a background in IT as a Systems Analyst and a Web Designer.

She has worked for over ten years supporting some of the most vulnerable people in society: people with learning disabilities and those who are physically and/or mentally handicapped, assisting them to achieve their maximum possible independence and encouraging them to becoming the best they can be. Her passion is in motivating people to realise their full potential.

Looking at these precious people living every day dealing with the challenges they face, Tracey often questioned what purpose they could possibly have in life. Along with her work experience and her own personal challenges she has grown to understand that *every* life is valuable; every human being is an individual with a purpose in this life because every life is God-given.

Tracey is passionate about purposeful living and believes that there is much more to life that we can discover in each individual once we make it our goal to find it.

Endorsements

Tracey Muponda's book *'Purpose, Provision and Power – discover the keys to unlock the path to your destiny'* does exactly what it says on the cover; it offers you a series of keys to inform and prepare you to embark on the journey to your destiny.

As you navigate your way through the truths presented within this book, you'll find Tracey's inspired words acting as a supportive and valued friend who wants nothing more than to see you succeed at being and doing all God has called you to. That doesn't mean she won't challenge you like any good friend would – to quote: "Heaven is pregnant with gifts God has given to His children. Ignorance is no excuse."

So, if you are wondering whether you have purpose, provision and power or if you need encouragement and support on your journey, then this book is for you. As Tracey writes, "Nothing merely exists for the sake of existing," and that includes you.

Sprinkled with inspirational anecdotes, scriptures and truth about our need to be connected to God for destiny, the chapters and sections are easy to read and guide you through the fundamentals to discover and unlock the path to your destiny.

This book by Tracey Muponda will confirm and remind you that you have a purpose; God has designed you with power and ability to get provision and it's time to use your keys to unlock your destiny!

Rev. Jacqueline Peart
Founder, DCUD (Deep Calleth Unto Deep)
Inspirational Speaker, Author, Poet, Trainer
www.jacqualinepeart.com

Is it really possible to say that all people are born for a purpose? Is it possible that we are actually born with the necessary gifts and talents to fulfil the dreams we hold? Could it really be possible that the answers to our most pressing needs and problems actually lie within us? And is it ever too late to discover this truth and have it working in our lives?

Tracey does a fine job to helps us answer these questions for ourselves (and more) through the pages of this book, and as a matter of fact I have taken up her book to be part of my own training material.

Kudakwashe Makombe
Facilitator for Personal Growth and Leadership
Breadwinners Network

"His divine power hath given unto us all things that pertain unto life and godliness, through the knowledge of him that hath called us to glory and virtue."

2 Peter 1:3

To the one who has made me and
has given me my true identity.

To the one who treasures me above
everything else and has given me the
reason to live.

To the one who has held me by
hand and has given me the strength
to get by each and every day.

To the one who will never let me
go, the one who is always there for
me.

To the one who loves me just the
way I am.

I dedicate this book to my Father
who is in heaven:

I love you, Daddy!

Contents

Foreword by Pastor Andrew Reed

It is both a privilege and an honour to write the foreword to Tracey's book 'Purpose, Provision and Power'. I have known Tracey along with her husband, Gwyn, and three children for many years. Tracey and Gwyn are a couple after God's own heart and as such are an incredible blessing to so many including my family and me. Tracey is a strong, discerning and humble Daughter of God, accomplished business woman and a dedicated loving wife and mother. God has used Tracey's experiences and closeness of relationship with Him to write this life-changing book.

Having read the book, my first thoughts were, "I need to read it again and other people must read it." 'Purpose, Provision and Power' is packed with so much spiritual truth; the more you read it the more I believe God will speak to you, and therefore the more revelation you will receive and the more you will grow. The book uses simple illustrations from everyday life and scenarios we can relate to or have experienced ourselves to enable the reader to understand powerful truths from God's Word. You do not have to work hard to read or understand the book, and therefore it is very easy for the Spirit of God to speak to you as you read. As with any good Christian book, Jesus is at the centre through the wealth of scripture that is present throughout and that the book is based on.

If you have been a Christian for some time, are just starting out on your journey with the Lord, or do not yet know Jesus as your Lord and Saviour, 'Purpose Provision and Power' will help you to understand that you have been created by a loving Heavenly Father who wants a relationship with you, wants to provide for you and desires for you to understand the meaning of life; that you are worth so much to Him and that He desires to care and provide for you; and that whatever is in your past or you are facing right now, God accepts you and wants to heal you and set you free to really live and enjoy life.

'Purpose, Provision and Power' will speak powerfully into your life providing Kingdom keys and spiritual truths to enable you to better understand your purpose and destiny in God and that you are no longer subject to sickness, poverty, worry, sin or anything else that may ensnare you; rather God, through His Word, has given you the power to take authority over those areas of your life that are not in line with His will for you as His child. If right now you are in the valley, on the mountaintop or somewhere in between, contained within this book is the truth of God's Word that will build your confidence in God and help propel you to the next season of your life, to have the understanding and faith to take the next step in your God given destiny.

God spoke to Jeremiah and said:

Jeremiah 1:5 (NIV)
Before I formed you in the womb I knew you, before you were born I set you apart; I appointed you as a prophet to the nations.

He later said to Jeremiah:

Jeremiah 29:11 (NIV)
"For I know the plans I have for you," declares the LORD, "plans to prosper you and not to harm you, plans to give you hope and a future."

God created you for a purpose and is ready to release to you all provision, having placed in you all power to achieve your life's calling. This book will help you tap into and access God's resources for your life.

In Deuteronomy, God spoke to His people and said:

Deuteronomy 30:19 (NLT)
Today I have given you the choice between life and death, between blessings and curses. Now I call on heaven and earth to witness the choice you make. Oh, that you would choose life, so that you and your descendants might live!

The Bible teaches that God is no respecter of persons, so in this context what He says to Jeremiah and to His people in Deuteronomy He is also saying to us; God has your destiny all figured out, but it is up to you to walk in it. You have a choice; this book will help equip you to make the right life choices and therefore prosper in God.

God has used Tracey's experience and testimony to enable this book to speak powerfully into your life. Wherever you are in life right now, don't miss out on God's goodness. As you read the book, ask

God to open your heart. He will speak to you and place you on course for the amazing future He has for you.

Equip yourself to make the right Spirit-led life choices, and help equip others to do the same by blessing them with this book.

Pastor Andrew Reed
Herts International Church

Acknowledgements

I believe there is always more than one person involved from the conception of a book to having it completed in print. I have had a team of wonderful people who have contributed to the making of this book a success. I therefore would like to give my special thanks to the following:

- My husband, Gwinyai, and our children, Rukudzo, Takomborerwa and Munesu, for the inspiration, motivation and support they gave me throughout the whole process of writing this book.
- My pastors, Dr Brad and Wyonna Norman, for the inspiration through their powerful, life-changing preaching and teachings.
- Rev. Jacqueline Peart and Mr Kudakwashe Makombe for the support, mentorship and guidance they gave.
- Hayley Bandy and Tina Carpenter for the great job they did in bringing the content together with grammatical corrections and making the book contents readable.
- The team at Onwards and Upwards Publishers who have done a wonderful job to make this book a success.

Thank you all.

Tracey Muponda
August 2013

Introduction

In life we often come across people who seem to have been born fortunate. They seem to have everything going for them. They may have been born in a well-to-do family, educated at the most prestigious schools and somehow just found a smooth way throughout their life. How can that be explained?

What made the rich man rich and the poor man poor? Where did man originate from? Has every man a set destiny? Some destined to live rich and joyous lives, others destined to live poor and miserable lives? Some healthy, others sickly, and some in the middle? If that be the case then we cannot do anything to change our lives. We will simply have to wait and see how life will turn out. We are no match for the creator of the universe and His divine plans.

If man is not in control of the circumstances in his life, then any attempt to do something about it will be in vain. Things will just turn out the way they were meant to.

However, when we have knowledge and understanding of the purpose of life, our views about life will shift, causing us to rise up and take responsibility for our present circumstances. We will seek to know the things freely given to us and learn how to release the power we have. We will feel empowered to do just that. The revelation of how valuable and loved we are will transform the way we view life.

This raises hope for a change: hope to see the good that we desire to see come to being; hope to see heaven on earth; and hope to find the answers that will unveil the so-called 'secrets' to a prosperous life we all long for.

I believe there is a well in each and every one of us – a well whose water seeks to flow out, to give life to those areas that we open and prepare to receive it. Water generally flows to where there is a platform to flow on, and it sinks into where there is room for it. It will reside where it can be contained. Where it is not prepared for, it just passes by.

Water has been given to serve all creation in this world, and each time it seeks to fulfil its purpose. We can put up barriers to resist its flow or create reservoirs to capture it for our own use. It is entirely up to us what we choose to do with it. But it has been provided to serve us and all creation. It has been given to us as an essential necessity. It is the essential ingredient that humanity, the plants, the animals, the fish cannot live without. Water, to us, is as necessary as the air we breathe. Without it there is no life.

Like water, air comes to us as a gift. It is available freely to all, just like the sun, moon and stars. They all have been provided freely as a gift from God the creator. All these – the rain, sun, moon, stars, air – are available to everyone. How we make use of them rests on us.

As a matter of fact, when we take a closer look at all the essentials in life we will see how they have all been abundantly supplied, without measure. There is more than enough air for everyone to take in, more than enough water to drink, more than enough sunlight and warmth for us all.

Isn't it interesting how we seem to have lost sight of the fact that we have been freely given the most important things that sustain life on earth? If God our creator gave us all these things freely, how much more of our daily provisions has He given? If He did not limit His supply of all these life essentials to you and me, why would He limit good health, riches, peace and joy? It is the power of His Word that holds the world together. It is His Word that keeps this world balanced and orderly, providing for every human need.

We are responsible for the measure of supply we demand on life by reason of choice. We all are called to fulfil a purpose. God knows all that we need, and He has abundantly supplied to all. I have never heard of anyone who had a sleepless night worrying about where he could get enough oxygen for himself and his family. No one takes the responsibility of ensuring the sun sets in order to rise the next day. No one ever worries about the law of gravity failing to maintain order on earth. God has set them to serve the earth and all its inhabitants. His power is active continuously to maintain the order of the universe.

The things we mostly worry about are those that we feel are too inconsequential for God to bother with, when we think we can take God out of a matter and make it our own. We may obtain good results to some extent; however, it is only with hard labour and toil that we can achieve. Some people think that worrying is a sign of taking responsibility. Now, if it is no big deal for God to supply the great things we need in life, how much more difficult can it be for Him to sort out the small and insignificant?

He is equally as concerned about every detail of our life. He knows the world in which we are living is capable of making those things which seem small and insignificant bigger than they really are, thus shifting our focus away from what really matters: our destiny. These hindrances can occupy our minds and distract us from seeing the mark set before us.

The reason why we have the ability to choose is simply to bring about those individual desires. We are all uniquely different, and we all have individual likings and tastes. Had we not been individually created, I'm sure things would have been just the same; we would have taken what was already there, like the bird that picks on what it finds on the ground.

The process of getting the things we truly want was never meant to be hard. Neither was it meant only for the chosen few. It was meant for all mankind, of every race, colour, nation or tribe to bring about, using the creative power within us without prejudice.

For us to impact the world and get onto the right path towards our destiny, we need to know our true divine nature. It is when we realise who we are that we rightfully position ourselves to become effective. We will begin to live life like never before. Our confidence and excitement of life will rise because we are doing the things that are true to our true nature.

In this book, I touch on how unique we all are. We all have a purpose to accomplish, and the very things we need in order to accomplish that purpose are locked within us. We have been structured and given power to enable us to get the job done.

To possess a thing without knowing it is as good as not having it. In the second part of this book, I discuss how much knowledge is required in order for us to utilise what we have. For knowledge to become effective we need to have understanding. When we understand our true nature and what we possess, we will then need this truth to become enlightened – to not only understand it but to see it as it really is. We need to acquire wisdom in order for us to apply the true principles to work for us.

Life is a journey with a destination. For us to get there, we need to gain access to set out on the right path.

This book will bring an enlightenment of how important it is for us to have knowledge of our true nature. With knowledge we should seek to understand because knowledge alone is just like holding a seed in your hand; as long as it remains in your hand it will produce nothing. When you acquire understanding, it will bring revelation that will expose those things available to us. Finally, the most important thing (without which all the knowledge we have revealed will come to nothing) is wisdom.

The Bible states that wisdom is the "principal thing". Wisdom will enable us to apply the knowledge we possess in order to bring about our desired outcome.

> **Proverbs 4:7-9**
> *Wisdom is the principal thing; therefore get wisdom: and with all thy getting get understanding. Exalt her, and she shall promote thee: she shall bring thee to honour, when thou dost embrace her. She shall give to thine head an ornament of grace: a crown of glory shall she deliver to thee.*

CHAPTER ONE

Why Was I Born This Way?

"Will I ever be able to marry, have my own wife and children? Why was I born this way? Do I have any purpose in life? Why am I different from all the other boys from school?" These are the kind of questions a certain boy of eight years used to ask. No one knew the answers to these questions; his parents couldn't answer him, neither could the doctors. He just couldn't figure out why he was born the way he was.

Maybe by finding answers, he would identify a solution to his worries... This young boy turned the questions to God, but there seemed to be no reply. No one could explain to Nick the reason he was born the way he was. There was no medical or scientific explanation. He often thought, "I don't want to be an outcast in life; I don't want to be a burden to my parents. I just want to live my own life doing the things I want to do."

Some of you may have heard about an incredible life journey of a man by the name Nick Vujicic – an evangelist, author, motivational speaker, and the director of the non-profit organization 'Life Without Limbs'. Nick was born in Melbourne, Australia, *without arms and legs.*

It was on December 4th, 1982, when Nick Vujicic was born. No one was prepared for what they were about to see – the shock of their life. His parents knew from the previous ultra-scans that their baby was a boy, but there had been no signs to indicate the lack of limbs. This was not only a shock to Nick's parents but to the whole medical team; nobody had expected anything like this.

When Nick's mother Dushka Vujicic had just given birth to her son, there was silence in the delivery room. Her husband, Boris Vujicic, who is a pastor, was also there in the delivery room awaiting the arrival of their baby. Imagine how it must have been for a mother who had just come out of birth pains, now waiting in anticipation to hold her baby for the very first time, to be greeted with an overwhelming period of silence. Like many mothers, Dushka was naturally expecting to be handed her child with a smile from the midwife. She expected to hear, "Congratulations, Mrs Vujicic. You have a healthy baby boy!" She knew what usually happened when a mother had just given birth because she was a midwife who worked as a paediatric nurse and had participated in many deliveries. In her case, her baby was instead handed over to a paediatrician for examination. Dushka immediately knew that something was very wrong. Then she heard her baby cry for the first time. For a moment Dushka was relieved that everything was okay... or was it?

In the meantime, Nick's father looked at his son and noticed that he had no arms. He felt weak with shock and anguish as he took another glance; the medical staff escorted him out of the delivery room. This was unbelievable; could he be seeing right? He was speechless. Unable to contain himself he walked right out of the delivery room hoping it to be a dream which he would wake out of and unsure of what to do next.

There was continued silence from the medical team. No one said anything to Dushka who sensed that something was very wrong. She could tell by the distressed looks on their faces.

"What is it?" she asked, but no-one answered. "What's wrong with my baby?" she insisted. The doctor then told her that her child had no arms and legs. Dushka wondered if she was hearing right.

How could a mother have taken such news? "That can't be!" she must have thought. "All the ultra-scans showed that everything was alright." Dushka had done everything she knew was right to have a healthy baby. What then had gone wrong? She began to cry and refused to hold him. It was a tough moment for everyone – for Dushka, for her husband and for the medical team. They didn't know how to handle it as everyone was in a shock.

How was their child going to survive in this world with this severe disability? It is natural for every parent to picture the kind of life their child would possibly live; how did Nick's mother and father picture his future?

Imagine the challenges Nick's parents had to face in order to incline people to regard Nick as an individual who just happened to have no arms or limbs but was no different from any other individual. Imagine how they felt when people would freak out at the sight of him. Imagine how the other members of the family reacted to the news when they heard it over the phone. "We have a son... but he doesn't have any arms or legs."

Nick's parents had to deal with several challenges. One was to accept the fact that their son was the way he was. Another was to be strong minded in mentoring their child to become strong and to accept himself the way he was; there was, of course, the possibility of Nick never coming to terms with the way he was for the rest of his life.

They had to soar above the norm and believe that even though Nick was disabled, he was capable of bringing the best out of who he was on the inside. And I believe that's why they made him go to school and gave him support and inspiration all the way. As much as they did their best, they only could do what they could – the rest depended on Nick, how he was going to look at life. However, the seeds they sowed into Nick prepared him to make the right decisions and he chose to accept himself the way he was.

That decision didn't come easily for him though. When he went to school, he began to feel the impact of his disability when he was often teased by other children. He felt lonely and very depressed. He struggled to find answers to his life's questions as the pressure from school mounted on him. At the age of eight he thought of committing suicide; he couldn't take more bullying. At ten years he tried to drown himself in a bath tub. What he now acknowledges is that God wouldn't let him die because He had created him for a purpose. His parents played a significant role in helping him see what was within him. His mother kept on reminding him that he was God's creation who was fearfully and wonderfully made. They encouraged him to get involved with other children to make known to them that being without arms and limbs didn't make him any different from them.

Nick often asked God why He had made him the way he was. At times he would get angry with God as he felt He was not answering him. That was until one day he read a certain passage in the scriptures about a man who was born blind. Jesus' disciples asked Him who had sinned that had caused the man to be blind:

John 9:3
Jesus answered, Neither hath this man sinned, nor his parents: but that the works of God should be made manifest in him.

That scripture ministered into Nick's heart. "Surely, if God had a plan for this blind man, he has a plan for me too," he thought to himself. This was his first turning point. His second turning point was when his mother brought him a story from a newspaper about a severely physically disabled man who was doing something to help other people. Nick began to realise that he could do something with his life. He started believing that God had a plan for him.

Instead of focusing on what he *didn't* have, he became grateful for what he *had* and determined to work hard in trying to do the things he wanted. How could he know he couldn't if he had never tried, his mother would challenge him.

From the moment Nick was born, I believe no one came even close to seeing the kind of man Nick was destined to become – a man mightily used by God to transform people's lives all over the world. Nick has accomplished amazing things, but he is still going, he is nowhere near to stopping. No one knew the kind of man he would be but God knew it all, and He knows exactly where Nick is going to be twenty years from now.

Nick may have some restrictions physically due to his lack of arms and legs, but who he is on the inside has already been defined by God our creator. The real Nick has no limitations or restrictions. What he's got has already been placed inside him for a purpose. It is given in the form of a seed which, when planted and natured, grows to reach its set destiny. The seed of greatness that was placed in him would naturally produce, if he just didn't restrict its development through focusing on his physical limitations, fear and doubt.

Many seek excuses to justify their unfruitfulness. For Nick it would have been very easy to just sit by and be confined to a wheelchair, not doing a thing about his life. I'm pretty sure he wouldn't even have felt guilty of being idle. It's also easy to assume that, realistically, no one would have expected him to do a thing anyway. But Nick demonstrated his determination and strong will by going for challenges that most of us wouldn't even dare to consider trying. He refused to just sit in his wheelchair and do nothing. His attitude is: whatever you want to do in life, do it; if you fail, do it again and again. What a great attitude to live by!

If we are to look around we can find many reasons for not doing what we are meant to be doing. This does not change our mission or purpose in life; it just moves us even further from the very things that we were created for – those things that would bring joy, fulfilment and freedom in our life. We are already here on earth; we have already been given life. God has already done *His* work. The plan has already been set, the purpose established, and the work is awaiting you and me to complete it. *Your* purpose is specifically for *you* to accomplish. No one can take your place, and no one can do the things you are meant to do exactly your way. God is counting on you to complete your mission.

What are you going to make with what you have been given? How about with the exceedingly abundant provision supplied, the riches of the glory (Ephesians 1:18) and the spiritual blessings (Ephesians 1:3)? What about with the exceedingly great power in you – the same power that raised Jesus from the dead (Ephesians 1:19)? You have been entrusted with them; why do you suppose this is? All are given for the accomplishment of a divine mandate.

Have you ever known people who seem to be angry every time you see them? They get angry at everyone and everything; they always find something to complain about. If it gets too warm they complain; if it gets too cold they complain; they complain about the government reform programmes; they complain about the high cost of living; they complain about lack of jobs, about the leadership; they complain about almost everything! Every misfortune they encounter is never their fault; there is always someone to blame. They often complain about things they don't have and often miss out on the most important gift they have: the precious gift of *life*.

God gave us all things to sustain the life He gave us. When eternal death had taken hold on mankind, God in His unending love and great mercy gave us His only son Jesus Christ to give us eternal life. We all have been adequately given the things we need. And it is our responsibility to utilise them.

Excuses, excuses!

From my own personal experience, there were times I had to perform tasks that required a little bit of stretching out of my comfort zone – such as exercising! I knew the benefits I would get afterwards. However, I would try to find excuses that would justify me from not exercising. By finding a good excuse, it would take away the guilt of not doing what I was supposed to do even though deep down I knew the right thing I should have done. I also knew very well that I really didn't want to exercise.

I believe most of us have an inner knowledge of the things we should be doing in life. To overcome taking on condemnation and guilt, many times we look for excuses that justify our not taking responsibility. Some people blame their childhood upbringing, others blame circumstance for their failures; some blame their lack of education, others blame their lack of money; some blame their nationality, others the colour of their skin. Some even hide behind the curtain of their religion and culture. We all need to realise what we have, embrace who we are, and quit looking to the physical things around us to facilitate our needs. Realising how thoroughly equipped we are will make us soar above any negative situation or circumstance that can ever come our way.

Who could have known that Nick would be touching millions of lives today? Nick is a perfect example that there is no excuse; we are all called for a specific purpose. Nick knows who he is and his true calling. He is using it for the glory of God. He understands that it's not God who caused his pain but that God always turns around things meant for evil for our good. Many broken lives are being mended because he refused to allow his physical limitations to stop him. He finds his source of strength in God. The knowledge of who he is and his faith in God empower him to do things which most of us wouldn't even dare to try. He can swim, surf, sky dive, play golf, play drums. He is truly amazing! He has been given such wisdom and a great sense of humour that inspires those who meet him. He is special just the way he is.

The seed of greatness within

Nick is a perfect example of the incredible power within us. That power, once released, breaks through every barrier of limitation. It is the power that we can control at our own will when we believe and release faith. It is not physical power nor the power from our arms and legs. Nick has found endless joy in his life in Jesus through this power. When he was asked how he managed to be happy despite having physical challenges, his answer was, "Knowing the truth of my value, my purpose and my destiny. Being thankful for what I do have instead of being angry for what I don't have. I have God on my side."

Can you imagine how it was for Nick when he felt he had no reason to live? From his physical outlook it is easy for us to imagine life as unbearable for him, but Nick lives *with purpose*. The power that is within him enables him to go for the things he desires to achieve.

Nick realised that his true value was not based on his physical outlook but on the person he was on the inside and all that had been entrusted to him to fulfil his divine destiny. Had he not found his true self, he may never have made any effort to learn surfing or sky diving or any of the incredible things he does. He may never have had the guts to marry his beautiful wife, and may never have become a proud dad of their lovely son. We may never have known about him. But we do, because he discovered the invaluable treasure he has within him.

We are equipped with everything we need to fulfil our purpose and reach our ultimate destiny in life. It does not matter who you are. The only limit is *you* – what you believe about yourself, what you see yourself achieving and your ability to challenge your fears of failure and insecurity. Nick refused to be confined to what his circumstances were imposing on him and chose to make the most out of what he had. His story is one of a kind that shows evidence that when we refuse to bow down to the limitations around us and find our purpose of living, nothing can stop us from achieving our destiny. The seed of greatness is within us. We walk carrying it every day; it is alive in us. Let us open the way for it to flourish by uprooting every hindrance for it to produce.

For more information, go to www.lifewithoutlimbs.org

CHAPTER TWO

Your Destiny in You

Every kind of seed has its destiny locked within itself. Unless one is a farmer or has planted seeds before, it is not easy to tell what kind of plant a seed will produce just by its appearance. One may be able to tell the kind of seed it is and visualise it based on what has been seen before; but truthfully, no one can tell exactly how its branches are going to be aligned or the exact taste of the fruit. One is able to tell the true nature of a seed only when it is planted, grows and produces fruit. For every tree is known by its fruit. (Luke 6:44)

My grandmother has an orchard of mango trees. Each mango tree produces mangoes that are slightly different from those of the other trees. Some produce very sweet mangoes, others not so sweet, while some produce more juice than others. One tree is always known for producing bitter mangoes. They are all planted in the same ground, in the same climatic conditions, and get the same nourishment; yet, interestingly, they all produce different-tasting mangoes. This reveals how uniquely different each individual is. That difference, which comes from within, is supplied by God our creator for a reason. It makes us individuals and differentiates us from the rest.

When one buys seeds from a supermarket, there is a picture on the packet. This picture shows the kind of fruits the seeds have the potential of producing.

Each seed has its potential in itself. No one can add anything to the seed to make it what it is not. Everything the seed needs in order to fulfil its destiny is locked within it. When a farmer buys seed, nothing starts happening until it is planted in the ground. The ground receives any kind of seed placed within it, and it holds and houses the seed. It gives the seed a foundation to stand on. It is the *type* of ground that varies and gives the seed its effectiveness of producing. If the ground is good for that particular seed, it maximises its effectiveness. If the ground is bad, it will limit the potential in the seed, which will die without realising its potential.

Seeds grow because they have living substance in them. Anything without life is dead and can never grow. There is a purpose for each life being lived today. We were brought into this world at this particular time because we were made for this time. What has been placed inside each of us living today is relevant for this time we are living. We have been brought into this world fully equipped for such a time as this. This phase of life we are in is just right for us. We all have a part to play and a solution to bring to this world.

Regardless of how insignificant it may seem, when we stand to do our own part we all work harmoniously towards attaining the ultimate goal of the creator of the universe. We are all different and unique, each in a special and significant way. I'm sure that believing we are insignificant displeases God. No one defines their true self but God. We have our identity in Him. He created us and equipped us for specific purposes.

Here are three fundamental principles about seeds:

- **Purpose.** Every seed is already named; it has its own established identity on the inside. It carries within it its clearly defined purpose to fulfil. It never changes its course. Its identity comes from its source.
- **Provision.** Everything required for the seed to achieve its destiny is already supplied and securely locked within itself. All the ingredients needed to make the seed develop are already provided. It is thoroughly equipped on its own. When we were created, God placed within us everything we would possibly require in order to achieve whatever needed to be accomplished.
- **Power.** Any kind of seed possesses sufficient power within itself to achieve its destiny. No-one can assist a seed to germinate. It has enough power to push its way out. That is the law of growth. We have our part to play and the seed does its own part. We can only hinder its growth when we step out

of line and do what we are not meant to be doing. Inside of us, there resides incredible power waiting to be released. That power is the creative power that can be released when we cooperate with God's set laws of creation.

God has set the universe in perfect order, governed by His established laws. These laws hold all creation in place and maintain perfect order in the universe. These are the laws that hold the stars in the sky; they maintain the climatic seasons, the seed time and harvest time; they cause the sun to rise and set without fail. When we work harmoniously with God's set laws, it establishes God's perfect plan for our individual lives.

Our part is to prepare the ground and create the right environment for the seed to grow. How we do that is through knowledge of the planting requirements and the process. We need to understand and apply the right principles for the seeds to be effective; otherwise, the seeds will die without producing anything.

No one can see life, no one can touch life, but we all see its effects. When people are alive, we see them walk, talk, hold their physical body, sleep and do what any living human being does. It is all evidence of the presence of life in them. The purpose of life is growth; one way or the other, we must see signs of growth in life. If one is not growing then it means one is dying.

It is this life that causes growth to our body, rejuvenates us, repairs any wounds, causes us to see and breathe the air around us. It causes a child to be conceived and grow inside the womb without any conscious effort.

As a matter of fact, everything our body has been created to do (without our conscious cooperation) it always does perfectly well as programmed by God, the giver of life. The life in us possesses enough power to continually pump the blood, day and night. The blood knows where to go. The white blood cells know exactly their purpose, as do the red blood cells. The vital organs required to sustain the body are already supplied and correctly positioned.

Everything required by the body to function has been provided. The power to perform is available. From each of the tiniest particles to the largest organs, all are created for a purpose. They each function to corporately accomplish that purpose. How that works is only known by God. Unless divinely revealed to us, no one can fully understand how the life in us causes our body to function the way it does.

However, with human input we see changes and adjustments to the functioning of the body. When we begin to deposit things that are not vital for the body we become ill, some organs fail to function to their optimum, or we become stressed, etc. When we deposit good, nourishing food to the body we get a healthy and happy body.

The issue here is that man has been given the capacity to have control over the affairs of his life. People have the freedom to choose whatever they want and follow it through. The battle we have to fight is to make the right choices and choose the correct way which leads to life.

This came into being when Adam and Eve sinned against God by disobeying His command. God had instructed them not to eat any fruit from the tree of the knowledge of good and evil. After eating the fruit, the Bible says that their eyes were opened. They knew they were naked (Genesis 3:7). Because of this knowledge they hid from God.

I personally believe Adam and Eve were clothed in God's glory, which enabled them to commune directly with God daily. And so, by eating the forbidden fruit, that glory departed from them and they saw themselves naked. As long as they were still in God's glory, I believe they would only have lived a holy and pure life without sin or any knowledge of it. God's glory provided a covering for them, which would have enabled them to effortlessly establish God's will on earth as in heaven. If they had not sinned, there would have been no place for sin. Evil would not have had any ground at all in this world.

The devil was not able – and he is still unable – to do anything without human cooperation. So, Adam's sin caused man to be separated from God, thus giving the devil a platform to operate in the world. As long as man was not clothed with the glory of God, the devil could establish his own plans against God's divine plans for mankind.

The devil came to take away all the good things God created for mankind to enjoy. But God, through Jesus Christ, took back everything the devil stole from Adam. We can now receive those things restored to us by grace through faith. I often see faith as an 'invisible arm' that we can use to take those things given to us by God. Those are things that we can't physically see, but we have knowledge of their existence because we believe God. This knowledge becomes so real within us that we 'know that we know' that we have them, and no one can take them away from us. Our faith causes us to reach out and take the things that we have been freely given by God, as the Bible describes faith as "the substance of the things hoped for, the evidence of the things not seen" (Hebrews 11:1). Just because something is not seen by our eyes does not mean it is not there, it just means it is not yet manifested in the physical realm. TV and radio waves are being transmitted around us even though we cannot see them.

So man has always been battling with two forces of influence: light and darkness. Following the way of light brings life, joy and peace. But the way of darkness always brings death, fear and worry.

Because of our nature we have our part to play. If we do not feed the body it will die. If we do not clothe it, it will be exposed. If we do not educate our mind we will remain in darkness. We need knowledge to understand through revelation the right things to do, to correctly nurture our bodies. With understanding we require wisdom to correctly apply that knowledge.

We need to know the right foods to eat that will nourish our body, we need to cover our body to keep warm, and we need to get the right information to get the right things in life. Cooperation with the creator is to live in accordance with the way He has already set for us. Any other way and we will only drift from the perfect life that has already been set for us.

We are all products of our Source, who is God. He created us uniquely for different purposes. He has equipped us with everything necessary to achieve these purposes and has empowered us to become whom He called us to be. Our ability to produce fruit does not depend on anyone; we are capable of becoming what God desires us to be. However, we need to have knowledge and to understand the nature of our being. We need the Spirit of God to reveal to us our identity and the wisdom of how to unlock the path to our destiny.

CHAPTER THREE

Your Purpose is Predefined

All things that we see have their origins from the source. They all started from the mind of the creator. We can begin to look at the world around us and everything in it, even the chairs we sit on. They were all completed in the creator's mind before they ever materialised. When we take a closer look at all of creation we realise that all things have a significant purpose in life.

Nothing merely exists for the sake of existing. In reality, every seemingly insignificant thing works together in perfect harmony, each fulfilling its purpose. A tree does what it's supposed to do, as do the flowers, birds, animals, sea creatures, etc. Man is the only being created as an individual who is capable of deciding and choosing the things he desires in life.

God is the source of our origin. We have life in Him. We live, move and have our being in God.[1] We are able to choose and create the things we desire. Because of this ability, if we make the wrong choices we end up on the wrong paths that lead to pain, sorrow and destruction. When we make the right choices, however, we end up in righteous ways of life, joy and peace.

God has allowed us to manage our own environment. All basic things have already been given to man. It is up to us to use them to our own liking. However, ignorance has been man's greatest enemy. It has kept him for a very long time in darkness, under the illusion of being imprisoned by his circumstances.

---

[1] Acts 17:28

A car manufacturer sets out to manufacture a heavy goods vehicle (HGV) for the purpose of transporting heavy loads. With this purpose in mind he spends hours, days, weeks and even years making plans that he can implement in order to make it possible. First, he finds a strong material that is able to sustain the heavy weight of the goods intended to be carried. He designs every detail of that vehicle based on the purpose for which it is being made. The metal you see on a truck is specifically designed to be able to withstand the heavy loads the vehicle will carry.

The vehicle is carefully fashioned in every single detail to eliminate any area of weakness. The engine is constructed to generate enough energy to be able to move the weight of its intended purpose. If the engine power is not high enough, regardless of how strong the vehicle structure is, it will not move. The manufacturer first makes sure every detail of the vehicle is carefully planned before going ahead with manufacturing. He knows his work; the vehicle only waits to become what is in the mind of the creator. When the HGV is ready, it is set to fulfil its purpose. If the user does not know how much the vehicle is capable of handling, it can be underutilised or overused.

So it is with every individual created. God has carefully designed and fashioned us according to the nature of His purpose for us. No one instructed God how tall a person was to be, or what talents should be placed within him. All we have been created for was to the best of God's intentions. However, we do have power to choose the path we are going to follow in our life. God is always waiting and willing to enlighten us when we choose to follow Him. He does not expect us to do the things we are not capable of, nor to give what we do not have.

Every child is born naked, holding nothing in his hands. This only means the world is open to him to create his own life blueprint; it does not mean he has nothing in him. He has *life* in him, and that life will cause him to grow and develop physically. We all have our gifts, callings, talents and potential within us in seed form.

Man already has the creative ability within him to bring something from the unseen. Just imagine what caused man to come up with a plan to generate electrical energy. What caused men to believe they could create light to shine in the dark? What gave them the courage to persistently follow that idea through until light bulbs were finally established? Where did men get the wisdom to use certain materials to enable electrical energy to flow into households? This all makes me realise how great and powerful the things are that God has placed in us. I believe every one of us has a seed for something very significant to contribute in a lifetime.

In Genesis, God said:

Genesis 1:26
Let us make man in our image, after our likeness: and let them have dominion over the fish of the sea, and over the fowl of the air, and over the cattle, and over all the earth, and over every creeping thing that creepeth upon the earth.

When God created man He clearly defined his role on the earth. The stature of men was perfect in order to achieve the mandate God had set before him. God knew all the equipment Adam would require to effectively perform his work, and God supplied all of it.

God had a reason and purpose for creating man in His own image, and He formed him after His likeness. He created man to represent Him and extend His Kingdom on the earth. He gave us the responsibility to fill the earth and bring it under our subjection through God's power working in us. The earth was created to be an extension of heaven, where man brings God's will to the earth just like it is in heaven. How was man going to be able to bring the things that are in heaven and establish His will on earth, but by God's eternal Spirit revealing heaven to him?

God gave us dominion over His creation. In Genesis 1:28, He blessed the man and said:

Genesis 1:28
Be fruitful, and multiply, and replenish the earth, and subdue it: and have dominion over the fish of the sea, and over the fowl of the air, and over every living thing that moveth upon the earth.

God has a purpose for your life. He has empowered you and provided you with everything you will need in order to accomplish it. You already have everything you may be looking for today. It is within you. However, ignorance is man's greatest enemy, which has kept him from discovering himself, what he has and what he can do.

Ever since Adam lost his dominion over the earth to Satan, a battle has been raging in man's mind. Jesus came as a light into the world to reveal the liberating truth to man, and to restore everything

31

Adam lost in the garden. The devil, on the other hand, is working tirelessly to keep man in darkness. He works by misguiding people from the truth through their mind. Every battle is won or lost in the arena of your mind. We are urged to control our mind:

> **2 Corinthians 10:5**
> *Casting down imaginations, and every high thing that exalteth itself against the knowledge of God, and bringing into captivity every thought to the obedience of Christ.*

Different situations we face in life may cause us to spend much of our time focusing on them to the extent that they seem larger than they really are. In face of such situations, we may feel powerless to overcome, and because we will be focusing more on them than on God, they seem to be enforce themselves above our knowledge of who He is. These disempowering thoughts often alienate us from the good that was created for us. They are untrue things that we have embraced in our life as the truth.

Looking at God's word, we learn that we have been put in a place of power, authority and dominion. It is when we experience things like failure, pain or shame that we start to believe certain things that are not true. Once they get grafted into the mind, they form beliefs that place boundaries and limits to what one can do. These beliefs will often be the cause of our decisions and actions. They battle against the true knowledge of God. Unless they get broken and replaced by the truth, thus causing our mind to be renewed, we will not be able to enjoy the freedom we have in Christ Jesus. Thus there are people who are saved yet still continue to fight the same battles over and over again. If we do not control our own thoughts, they will enslave us and so become dominated by different storms in life.

The hope of His calling

When you receive a phone call from someone, there is normally a reason for the call. They may just want to find out how you are or give you some information. It is the same with God. He did not just *call* us to be righteous; He *made* us righteous in order to qualify us to gain access into His presence. He has a reason for our existence. Our mandate is to seek to find out what God intends to achieve through us. Everything exists for a purpose.

Ephesians 2:10
For we are his workmanship, created in Christ Jesus unto good works, which God hath before ordained that we should walk in them.

One of the reasons for our existence is to enforce the governance of God's Kingdom over all His creation by our dominance. Jesus did just that during His ministry on earth. He established God's will wherever He went, restoring divine order in the lives of people who were willing and available. We are expected to walk like Jesus did. What could the reason be for Jesus telling us that we could also do the works He did, and greater works, if it was not God's intended purpose for us? Why would we have been given so much power to overcome every force of evil? God created us to establish good works wherever we go. If you want an example of good works, look at Jesus' life on the earth. Examine how He fulfilled His Father's plan and purpose. He did His Father's will. He only did what He saw His Father do. Jesus received instructions from God and accomplished His mission.

The Kingdom within

Luke 17:21
Neither shall they say, Lo here! Or, lo there! For, behold, the kingdom of God is within you.

Man is continuously searching for the Kingdom that is already within him, whether he knows it or not. The reason for the search is the realisation that there is a place of safety, a place of peace, a place of provision, a place of power that we crave for, a place of fulfilment which we have not yet grasped. This is a place where our purpose is found; it is where the very things men are tirelessly seeking are found; it is where the incredibly creative power lays dormant.

Jesus commanded us to seek first the Kingdom of God and explained that everything else shall be added to us. Everything we need is in God's Kingdom. His kingdom is about establishing His will on the earth just as it is in heaven. That kingdom is not far or out of reach for anyone. It has been put within men to establish it on earth.

Most of us seek what we already have within. The reason for feelings of restlessness, confusion and hopelessness for many is that they are searching for what they do not really know. Their heart is longing for something it knows is missing in their life. People go to great lengths trying to find that which they are longing for, but they search in the wrong places. This only results in anger, frustration, unfruitfulness and desperation. Our utmost goal in life should be to seek the Kingdom of God, for when we find it we find everything else that we are searching for, day and night. Discovering the Kingdom within you is the key that will unlock everything else in your life.

Jesus said, "Seek first the kingdom of God..." because He knew it was the only way of unlocking the path to your destiny. When you start searching for something you know that it is there somewhere. Through persistence and determination, you will usually only stop when you find it. This is dependent upon how important the thing you are seeking is to you. If you know that your life depends on it, you will search for it with all your being. The amount of energy you put into it is determined by your knowledge of its importance.

Yes, men are searching for the true meaning of life. They are seeking ways in which they can be in control. Until we find that Kingdom, life will continue to seem worthless and insignificant. Many will continue to live as victims of the evil forces of this world.

We need to know the things that we have been freely given. We need to have the knowledge of God in us and of His perfect will for us. However, knowledge alone will not do us any good; we need to be able to understand the knowledge we receive. When we gain understanding, it brings enlightenment of the deeper meaning of life, bringing revelation to us. Our ultimate goal in life is to get wisdom. Wisdom is what will enable us to make the right decisions and choices. By wisdom, God created all things great and small.

We may find ways of making up for the deep longings of our heart, but it will only be a matter of time until we realise that what we thought we needed was actually not what we have worked so hard to get.

Many have believed that through becoming rich they would find what they need. But as the years have passed by and they have become wealthy they have still found no fulfilment in their lives. Some people have gone to great lengths, even selling their souls to the devil, in the hope of finding what can only be found in the Kingdom of God. Many have moved from religion to religion, from church to church; some have been in and out of marriages – but still have not found what they are looking for. People are continuously searching for the reason for their being. Many have sacrificed so much in life in order to earn their desired lifestyle. Their need for recognition, to have power and to control their environment has caused some people to take action that has actually moved them further away from the Source of all things.

What we need to realise is that we have God's Kingdom within us. In this Kingdom is everything we need to be fulfilled and satisfied in life. If we found the Kingdom, we would see that everything else in life is hinged on it.

Romans 14:17
For the kingdom of God is not a matter of eating and drinking but of righteousness and peace and joy in the Holy Spirit.

There is more to God's Kingdom than just food and drink! It is through God's Kingdom that He has provided us with the purpose and power to reach our destiny.

Man an eternal being

Man is an eternal being. God breathed His breath of life into us, making us a living soul. God's breath energised man's physical being, which enabled him to be connected to the physical world. It is the breath of God (often called the spirit of man) that is responsible for ensuring that our body functions properly.

Acts 17:28
In Him we live, move and have our being.

Through our body we are able to feel, touch, hear and smell things in our physical world. The body is set to connect and respond to the physical nature. When it is cold, our brain receives information from our body that it is cold, and our brain is able to interpret it and take action in response. The body depends on the information it gets from the physical world. Many of us have been trained most of our life to quickly respond to the demands of the body in fulfilling its needs; yet we totally ignore the need to feed and nurture our inner man (our spirit). This has given our body more dominance and control over much of the affairs of our life.

It is through the spirit that we can control our body and put it into subjection. Just like any other physical creation, our physical body does not understand the language or things of God, because they function on different planes. The body can relate to things that can potentially cause pain, discomfort, insecurity, unfamiliarity or anything it is not accustomed to. Its natural reaction is to resist it. However, when we understand that our body does not understand spiritual things, we can determine to develop our spiritual senses in order to be in control. Failure to do this has been the root cause for all sickness, sadness, frustrations, fears and worries in people's lives.

On the other hand, our spirit is from God, therefore we are one with God; we have the power of God within us. God first created man by His spoken Word; then He formed him and fashioned his being with His hands:

> **Genesis 2:7**
> *And the LORD God formed man of the dust of the ground, and breathed into his nostrils the breath of life; and man became a living soul.*

Of everything God created, man was the only creature He took time to use His hands to form. This should speak volumes as to how special we are in His sight. For most of creation, God spoke and they came into being, but for man He created him in stages. Firstly, God had a vision of how He would create man, and then He created him through His spoken Word.

When God spoke man into existence, He had a clearly defined purpose for him. Man was created in God's image: his outlook, structure and form. An image takes the exact external form of the structure it represents. When we speak of man being created in God's image, we are not referring to our physical outlook. We all know that God is spirit. We take after God's image and likeness in our spirit. The spirit of man takes the image and likeness of God. How, then, can we know what man looks like on the inside? God is spirit and man is spirit and neither can be seen with our physical eyes. We can, however, know what man really looks like by looking into God's Word.

> **James 1:23-24**
> *For if any be a hearer of the word, and not a doer, he is like unto a man beholding his natural face in a glass: for he beholdeth himself, and goeth his way, and straightway forgetteth what manner of man he was.*

James likens the Word of God to a mirror. By taking a look at ourselves in the mirror we get to know how we look. So when we go out we can walk in confidence in the knowledge of our appearance. If anyone should say, "Hey, there is a massive spot on your face," it is natural to go and find a mirror to see whether the person is telling the truth or not. A mirror has a function – to reflect your image back to you – and so does the Word of God; it reflects our spiritual image back to us. 'Holding on to the Word and living by it' means living in the conscious knowledge of who we are in God. We can relate to the Word of God as our spiritual mirror, which shows us our true nature and identity according to our Father, the creator.

Another way of saying that we were created in God's image is to say that we have His *likeness*. I am sure many of us have come across the expression 'like father like son'. It means being similar in nature or resembling the original form. We have the nature of God in us. God is a creative God and we are like Him; we too are creative. We can create something out of nothing just as God does. The Bible tells us that He made us gods on this earth:

Psalm 82:6
I said, 'You are gods, sons of the Most High, all of you.'

Through us, God wants to extend His heavenly Kingdom on earth. Every human life is valuable to Him; we are eternal beings, just like He is. The spirit that lives in us came from God. From His infinitely abundant being, He imparted His power into us. At the end of human life on this earthly plane, everything will return to its source: dust to dust and spirit to spirit.

As an aside, when Adam sinned he was separated from God and so was every man. However, Jesus Christ came to reconcile man back to God; so we are again united with God when we are born again. Our physical bodies will die and return to dust, but our spirit will live on forever.

The reason for our being

I believe every single person has had a moment (or will have a moment) in life when they will search for the utmost reason for their being in this world. Unfortunately, for some it will be while taking stock of their life while on their deathbed. By then they will feel regret if they have lived an empty and unfulfilled life and will wish they could have done something worthwhile with it. Everyone is in search of dominance, whether we realise it or not. We all want to be in control of our environment and every area of our life. Frustration and hopelessness can come when we feel overpowered and out of control of our environment. This is simply because *that is who we are*. We cannot search for what we have never had. If you lose your car keys, you search because you know that you had them before. You cannot search for something you really know is non-existent.

When God created us, He gave us dominion over the whole of creation. He gave that command in our spirit when He commanded our creation and spoke out our mandate upon the earth. It is why we are all in search for something greater. Sometimes we may not realise what it is we are really searching for. Some think they will find it when they achieve a certain academic level, others think they will find it when they become rich; some think they can find it by using drugs, and others when they finally find their soul mate. Upon getting whatever it is that they thought would bring fulfilment to their life, they still find themselves unfulfilled.

God gave us the power to extend His heavenly Kingdom on the earth. It was His purpose for us to rule over the affairs of the earth and so He gave us every provision within our spirit for us to reign. The heavenly Kingdom is that of the knowledge of God – His divine plan for us and the releasing of His power to fulfil divine destiny.

God is a God of plan and purpose. Whatever He creates, He designs it in accordance with (and to fulfil) a divine purpose. He created a perfect environment suitable for every kind of creature, great and small. He made the waters of the sea for the aquatic creatures, the birds with wings to fly. The ability of every creature is within the creature itself. No one has ever taught a bird to fly, or fish to swim, or the lion to hunt for food. Somehow, they always find their way to fulfil their destiny. A bird kept in a cage can never lose its ability to fly. Regardless of how long it has been kept there, should an opportunity arise, it will fly away.

I'm sure in our daily lives we have come across situations that seem so out of our realm that at times we find ourselves with more of a defeatist attitude than a victorious one. Though I have been a Christian a long time, I am often faced with decisions to make regarding every challenge I face – whether to give up or to trust God's Word to work for me. When any kind of situation arises, we go through certain emotional struggles to try to figure out the nature of it. Often we need to make decisions of some kind. We are always faced with situations that require us to make choices, whether to do it God's way or our own way.

What influences our decision is the knowledge we have of God and how we interpret each situation. Earthly knowledge will consider physical evidence; the things we have learnt may be from other people's experiences or our own experiences. Divine knowledge is God-given and God-inspired. It is revelation knowledge that gives us confidence in God's willingness and ability to enable us to be victorious. Regardless of what the evidence around us may be suggesting, divine knowledge sees beyond the natural and reveals things as they really are in the spirit.

Imagine if you had the power to achieve anything you wanted and you had everything you needed to make it happen. Imagine you knew exactly what you had to do. Think of how different your life could be right now. What could you have done differently from what you are doing right now?

Many of us have been held back because of a lack of knowledge of the essential ingredients of our life. We have not been doing the things we were called to do because we simply did not have the knowledge.

Here is the prayer that the apostle Paul spoke:

Ephesians 1:17-19
...That the God of our Lord Jesus Christ, the Father of glory, may give unto you the spirit of wisdom and revelation in the knowledge of him: The eyes of your understanding being enlightened; that ye may know what is the hope of his calling, and what the riches of the glory of his inheritance in the saints, And what is the exceeding greatness of his power to us-ward who believe, according to the working of his mighty power.

God is the God of the universe. However, He gave the earth to men. He gave us the power to rule. Jesus said that the Kingdom of God is within us. We are carriers of His presence and enforcers of His dominance over the affairs of this earth. God can alter the course of nature when we gain knowledge of our purpose, power and provision in this world. Elijah prayed that it would not rain and it did not rain for about three years. Fire lost its power when the three Hebrew men Meshach, Shadrach and Abednego were thrown into a burning fiery furnace. Elisha caused a borrowed iron axe head to float when it had fallen into the water. Through Moses, God caused sea waters to open and make way for the children of Israel to pass through. Through us, God's unlimited power can be demonstrated to control the forces of nature and any kind of environment. We only need to have an understanding of how the Kingdom principles work.

The spirit world created the physical world. The way God designed us is to connect the spirit world to the physical world. We are able to create things from the spirit into the physical.

CHAPTER FOUR

Provision

Kingdom providence

2 Peter 1:2-3

Grace and peace be multiplied unto you through the knowledge of God, and of Jesus our Lord, according as his divine power hath given unto us all things that pertain unto life and godliness, through the knowledge of him that hath called us to glory and virtue.

God has made available to us all good things we require in order to live a godly life here on earth. Everything that we would ever need in this life, God has already supplied. How we are to obtain them is by the knowledge of God. Without knowledge of your entitlement, you can never claim the inheritance which was left for you.

In the UK government funds, there has been an estimated figure of £15 billion of unclaimed financial assets just lying there.[2] Does it mean the deceased people who owned these assets had not even one heir? Of course they did; but how many people are suffering whose lives could have been changed had they known that a relative had left so much money and they were heirs to it?

There are now agencies that work to help people discover if there is any inheritance that may have been left by an unknown uncle or aunt. Many people are benefiting from the inheritance of their relatives they never saw. They may be fifth or sixth in line, but it

---

[2] See *www.uar.co.uk/help/aboutlostassets.* Experian is a global information services company for the Unclaimed Assets Register.

doesn't matter. All that matters is, somewhere along the blood line they were related to the deceased.

In Matthew 6:25-34, Jesus told His disciples not to be worried about tomorrow regarding what they were going to eat, to drink, or to wear. He stated that there were many more important things such as life and the body itself.

Worry is a self-destructive weapon. It focuses over and over again on the problem – thinking about it and seeing everything that may seriously go wrong as a result. Worry never sees victory; it sees destruction, failure, shame and torment. The source of worry is the spirit of fear, which is the kingdom of darkness at work.

Worry will totally black out or diminish the power of God's Word. It is impossible to see God's ability and willingness to deliver you with a worrying mind. It will not produce any good fruit; it will produce the things feared and ill-health. Some medical practitioners believe that many diseases can be stress-related. Many people are worried about future insecurities reported in the media. Many now overwork their bodies with little rest in order to feel secure about tomorrow.

Here, Jesus was teaching His disciples and giving examples to illustrate the lesson that God knew the things they had need of. It was not about earning a living. The life we have today, we did not earn. Why, then, should we think that we have to earn it now? He explained to them the fundamentally important issues in regard to provision, the Kingdom of God and His righteousness.

It is as if Jesus is saying (my own paraphrase), "Guys, you are wasting your life away on the things that are supposed to be effortlessly flowing to you. And because of this, you haven't got time to focus on issues that matter most. The reason why you are worried is because you are applying the wrong method to obtain your necessities. There is a much easier way: just commit yourself to seeking the Kingdom of God. Upon discovering the Kingdom, you will also discover the easy way of obtaining what you are seeking. For everything you need is in the Kingdom."

The Kingdom is not far away. No one can say it is out of reach. It is found within each and every one of us. Once you find it, it is the way that will bring you everything else you desire. All things that you need are already waiting for you to take.

Jesus urges us to take into account the lifestyle of the birds; they do not sow nor reap, and yet our heavenly Father feeds them. God made provision for all creation. He is our Father; how can He faithfully feed the birds and clothe the lilies of the field and forget about us? Is it possible? This is what Jesus said in verse 26:

Matthew 6:26
...are you not more important than they?

I am not suggesting that people should not go to work or that they should just stay at home praying all day. That is not my point. My point is this: we should not work to earn a living; instead, we should work to fulfil divine purpose. That means finding the things you are passionate about and doing them as your act of service to God. God has provided everything this world needs by giving everyone a role to play. If everyone were to discover what their right path is, we would all work corporately towards fulfilling God's ultimate goal, which is to bring heaven on earth. Make every day count! Wake up feeling good and look forward to yet another day! How can that be possible when one knows for sure that they absolutely hate the job they will be doing for the next eight hours? How much gratitude can come out of that?

There is a better way to live. Earning a living is not the way. Rather, knowing what we have and releasing it to ourself is the way. God has provided everything necessary to enable us to enjoy our life. It is all found in the Kingdom of God, which we are carrying within us everywhere we go. We can only start releasing it with the knowledge of it.

The riches of the glory

God has already made provision for every one of His purposes to be accomplished. No one can stand before God's throne on Judgement Day to give the excuse that he did not have enough to accomplish his mission. God will one day ask us what we did with what has been entrusted to us. How are we going to answer? "I didn't know" or "I didn't have enough" or "I didn't get a chance"?

What is going to be your answer? It is worth finding some quiet place by yourself to consider where your life is right now. It really does not matter if you are twelve years old or eighty years old. It is not where you start but how you finish. Tomorrow is in the future; it may never come. Be determined to find out what it is that you have been given and how you can use it to bring the Kingdom of God *today*. How you spend eternity and your eternal position is dependent on what you did with what has been put in your hands.

No one will be justified in standing before God and telling Him how unfair He is for giving so-and-so a higher rank to rule. Our works on earth will testify for us. The Bible tells us that our works are going to be tried with fire.

Let this be an encouragement for us all to rise up from where we are. We must realise what is in us in order to get onto the right path and, thus, fulfil our divine destiny.

God has promised a supply for every need:

> **Philippians 4:19**
> *But my God shall supply all your need according to his riches in glory by Christ Jesus.*

While growing up in a life of struggle, I really had a hard time believing this scripture and applying it to my own life. When Jesus was teaching His disciples to pray in Matthew 6:9-13, He told them to ask God to give them their "daily bread". He was talking about asking for daily provision. I believe that what Jesus said then to His disciples He would say to us again today. For the laws of God's Kingdom do not change.

By making a habit of asking God for our daily provision, it gives us an awareness of God's providence and care for us each and every day. It gives us the confidence of having God take care of all our needs. God wants you to focus on more important things in your life. He wants us to leave the worries of tomorrow for tomorrow to sort out. He wants us to enjoy each day with a grateful heart. He urges us not to worry about tomorrow (Matthew 6:34). Worry always has to do with what may come next, never about what has already happened.

We were not created to only work for food, clothing, to pay bills, the mortgage and so on; then, after we have worked all our life, we retire, hopefully having paid up all our mortgage and wait until the Lord takes us home. Hope for eternal life should motivate us and keep us focused on the good things waiting for us when we pass on! It strengthens us to know that when we are surrounded by darkness there is light in Jesus awaiting us. The Bible calls hope the anchor of the soul:

Hebrews 6:19
We have this hope as an anchor for the soul, firm and secure...

Every born again child of God will have eternal life in God's glory. But how you conduct your life on earth will determine your eternal reward. In the parable of the talents in Matthew 25, Jesus illustrated how seriously God takes what we do with what He has given to us, as follows.

A certain master had three servants and gave each of them talents: five, two and one respectively. I am sure this master knew his servants' abilities very well and so he gave the talents based on that. The servants given five and two talents each gained more from what they had. But the servant who was given only one talent never did anything with it; instead, he had reasons he thought would justify his inability to produce. One of the reasons, he confessed, was that he was afraid.

Because of the reasons, he stored his talent in an unproductive place. What he did not realise was that it was not the master's intention to benefit from it. It was a way of proving his worthiness and faithfulness to the little he had been entrusted with. As a result, the master called his unfruitful servant wicked and slothful. His only talent was taken away and given to the fruitful servant and he was cast away. The master said to his fruitful servants:

Matthew 25:23
Well done, good and faithful servant; thou hast been faithful over a few things, I will make thee ruler over many things: enter thou into the joy of thy lord.

God has made the riches of His glory available to us for a reason. He will not expect us to give what we do not have. But what we have He does not want us to sit on. This is a serious matter to God. Jesus said that any branch in Him that does not bear fruit, He takes away. Still the question stands: what are you going to do with what you have been given?

The riches of God's glory come to us as bags of seeds. These seeds are His Word, which Peter describes as the incorruptible seed that lives and abides forever:

1 Peter 1:23
*Being born again, not of corruptible seed, but of incorruptible,
by the word of God, which lives and abides for ever.*

These words are like power containers which carry life, power and purpose. God has given us the riches of His glory all wrapped in His Word. There is no other way of accessing these riches except by His *Word.* That is why Jesus said in John 14:6 that He was the way, the truth and the life; no man can get to the Father except by Him.

The absolute seed supplied

God's word is absolute. It is perfect, complete and total. It is referred to as an incorruptible seed that lives and abides forever, in 1 Peter 1:23. Jesus said that the words He spoke were spirit and were life (John 6:63). This tells us that there is much more to words than just mere words. Every word we speak carries life within it. Words are power-containers; they produce the life they are intended to accomplish. Matthew 12:36-37 tells us that we are going to give account for every idle word spoken on the day of judgement and that we are justified or condemned by our words. This reveals to us how God holds us accountable for every word we speak – good or bad – and for what those words do to us. We should be careful with our speech and should not waste the power of word that has been entrusted to us by God our father.

For us, the Word of God is given and referred to in some passages of scripture as 'seeds'. We know what seeds do when they are planted; they produce after their own kind. It is the same with the word of God – it will do what it is intended to do.

Isaiah 55:11
*So shall my word be that goes forth out of my mouth: it shall not
return unto me void, but it shall accomplish that which I please,
and it shall prosper in the thing whereto I sent it.*

Every word that God has spoken carries the power to fulfil the purpose it is sent for. God has provided through His Word for any need or any circumstance that may arise at any time in your life. It is beneficial to always have the Word of God in us so that when situations arise we will be fully equipped.

God cannot lie. Whatever He has promised to give us through His Word is already a done deal. Through the set laws, every promise of provision we find in His Word has already been established. His Word is sure; it cannot change. He has established a way for us to get the things He has given to us. As long as we cooperate with these laws we will see ourselves living a delightful life.

John 1:1-5
In the beginning was the Word, and the Word was with God, and the Word was God. The same was in the beginning with God. All things were made by him; and without him was not anything made that was made. In him was life; and the life was the light of men. And the light shineth in darkness; and the darkness comprehended it not.

This scripture talks about the Word being in existence before everything else was created. It was the Word that created all things that were made – and that is still the case today; our words are still actively creating our world. There was life in the Word which was men's light. The purpose of the light is to overcome darkness. Light is more powerful than darkness. Where there is darkness, there is absence of life. Darkness signifies evil, sin, obscurity, night, ignorance and moral depravity.

Here we are being told that the light came and shone over sin, evil, ignorance, obscurity, night and moral depravity, but the darkness could not comprehend it. The darkness did not succeed in overcoming the light of Jesus. He came to become the light to us so that those who dwell in Him would never live in darkness (John 12:46). When we receive the light (Jesus), He gives us the power to become sons of God (John 1:12). When we are born again we become children of God, born into the family of God. However, through growth and maturity in Him, we become sons. Through Him we have been given the ability and the capacity to become the sons of God. We get the rights, privileges and authority any son can have over his father's affairs.

God sent the same Word that created the world to give life to us by overcoming the darkness. The Word will always produce its intended purpose. It never fails to accomplish what it is sent for.

One particular day, when I was battling to see victory in a very challenging situation I was facing, I felt the Lord saying, "My Word

is sure. If you keep holding my Word, your victory is also sure."
God's Word will always expose the lies of the enemy regarding any
circumstance.

> **Psalm 30:5**
> *For his anger endureth but a moment; in his favour is life:*
> *weeping may endure for a night, but joy cometh in the morning.*

I often wondered why it was that I had victory in some areas yet
defeat in others. The victory I got when I prayed for the sick and they
were healed and miracles I had seen God performing in my life gave
me unshakeable confidence that God was with us. But there were
certain areas that I really struggled in. I was still in darkness as far as
those areas were concerned.

When we get revelation of His Word regarding any particular
subject, this is when our 'joy in the morning' (victory) comes. Night-
time is a time of darkness; it is a time of sleeping that means no
action, a time of ignorance and stumbling. But morning time is a time
of brightness, revelation, clarity and activity.

God's Kingdom rules

> **Psalm 103:19**
> *The LORD hath prepared his throne in the heavens; and his*
> *kingdom rules over all.*

The Kingdom of God is where the influence of God is in action.
When we become born again, we receive Jesus as the Lord of our life.
Before this, we have been subjected to the evil one by the sinful
nature we inherited from Adam, and we have got to make a
transition to allow the rulership of God to have dominance over our
life. This is done when we are born again and are filled with the
knowledge of God's will.

Being born again into the Kingdom of God is one thing; living it is
another. We can be guaranteed eternal life but be living hell on earth.
God cannot do what we do not allow Him to do. It is the act of our
will and cooperation with Him that enables His power to be released
in our life. God said, "If you are willing and obedient you shall eat
the best of the land" (Isaiah 1:19). Notice it requires your willingness
and obedience to enjoy the best of the land. It's all already supplied,
but it's entirely up to you if you wish to benefit from it. We can only

obey what we know, and our willingness is our attitude towards God's instructions to us.

Jesus said, "The Kingdom of God is within us."[3] He didn't mean it was in some faraway place. He meant we are all filled with the power that brings all the joy, every provision, every kind of need we may have in our life; we have it in us. We have in us power to overcome any kind of challenge that may show up in our life. We have the power to control every circumstance surrounding us when we have perfect knowledge of the power in us.

Psalm 103:19
God's throne is in the heavens, but His Kingdom rules over all.

It is important to know that God's Kingdom rules over the whole universe. However, men choose what kingdom to be governed by in their individual lives. We can either receive the governance of God or deny it; we can live by its principle, or not. It is God's Kingdom that sustains the world. It still determines the times of the seasons. It still makes the sun faithfully come out in the morning and the stars at night. It is His Kingdom that still separates the seas from the dry lands. It is the one that still ensures that sowing time and reaping time will never cease as long as the earth remains. It is the Kingdom of God that enables the rain to fall on every land and the sun to shine.

The Kingdom of God is the ruling Kingdom of the whole earth. Yes, the devil took man's keys to rule over the affairs of this earth, but he did not create a thing. It is God who created all creation, not the devil. The devil uses people's authority to bring about his evil schemes. Without human cooperation (through deception) the devil has absolutely no power at all. That is why he uses every trick to get man off track and away from God's plans for him.

We should remember that Satan used to be a powerful angel of the Lord. He saw how God operated and thought he could be like Him. And so it only takes God's power to overcome him. Our own efforts and strength can never withstand against the devil; he is powerful. God knew that, which is why He gave us the Holy Spirit's power to overcome him. So the Kingdom of God rules over all.

---

[3] Luke 17:21

The Bible likens the Kingdom of God in us to a hidden treasure, which we must seek to find. The good news is that God hid it for us – from our enemies, not from us.

Jesus said:

Luke 12:32
Fear not little flock, it is your father's good pleasure to give you the kingdom.

He wants us to find it for our own good. We need our mind renewed by the Word of God, in order to know the perfect will of God. Everything we need is in the Kingdom of heaven. God wants His will to be done in this world as it is done in heaven. With His power at work through us we make it happen. God needs us to extend His Kingdom on the earth. He has restricted Himself from worldly affairs. Man has been given the legal right to operate and influence both the physical and the spiritual realm.

God has chosen to work through human cooperation in worldly affairs. Man has a part to play and so does God. Jesus had to manifest as the Son of Man in order to restore men back to God. God worked through Moses to deliver His people from the bondage they were under in Egypt.

He clearly gave man dominion and power to be the ruler in the world, and man handed it over to the devil through being deceived. However, Jesus came to get the keys and gave them back to the sons of men to restore divine order on earth. The Bible says that we are kings and priest. One can only be a king if one has a domain to rule over.

CHAPTER FIVE

Power

The power in us

People are becoming more and more aware of this incredibly irresistible power we possess. They need to know the kind of power they have and how to release it.

Each on of us has of the incredible, unlimited power within us to create whatever we choose. That is our true nature. Earth was created for man and God made every provision for man to choose whatever he desired. What our mind conceives is not something physical that we can touch or feel; it is something in the spirit.

Jesus said:

Mark 11:24:
...whatsoever things you desire, when you pray, believe that you receive it. And you shall have them.

This reveals God's willingness to fulfil every man's desire. Desire comes from the heart. Instead of just wishing our desires away because there is no way we can possibly see them happening, we just need to simply ask. We should not hesitate to ask God for the things we desire because they seem out of our reach. God has higher ways of doing things. He knows perfect ways of bringing your desires to you that you don't see. It is men who place limits on the self and not God.

Many of us have made the mistake of asking for those things we know we are capable of accomplishing ourselves. We have tended to play it safe in order to avoid being disappointed. Our physical ability will always be restricted by physical conditions, but when we depend on God's supernatural ability we will operate in the supernatural realm. This means taking our focus off ourself and focusing on God's infinite power.

You may ask, what if someone has an evil desire? Could that not be a dangerous statement? Ideally, before the fall of man, man's desire was just, pure and holy. Man's desire was from the Source of his being, which is God. Since our spirit came from God, man was to do the things that he saw in his spirit. He was able to draw from within him peace, love, health, provision, harmony, etc., without any resistance or struggle. Faith was part of man that was given effortlessly to create our own world.

However, when evil invaded the earth, the truth about God which was within man became distorted. Man now had conflicting choices: to be led by the influence from within (our spirit) or to be led by the influence from without (the flesh). This brought confusion in man and alienated him from God's plan and purpose for his being. Instead of being one with God and representing God in all his affairs, man found himself battling between two forces: the force of darkness, which is that of the evil one and ignorance, and the force of light, which is that of good and knowledge of the truth.

The force of darkness causes man to struggle aimlessly and lose the sense of his being. It causes man to be controlled and influenced by the physical world, instead of man influencing the physical world from the spiritual one. This has resulted in man conceiving evil desires and imaginations which have brought disasters and chaos in the world. Man is a creative being; whatever he can conceive in his mind, he can bring it to pass. Ignorance of this creative power has resulted in many being controlled by their circumstances yet God gave us the power to control them. It is all because of ignorance that man becomes overwhelmed by his circumstances.

In all this, God sent His son Jesus to restore man's dominance in the world. In Mark 11:22, before Jesus began teaching His disciples on faith, He said, "Have faith in God." This statement puts God at the centre of all things we want or desire to have. Faith originates from God. It comes by hearing His word; so, when we hear His Word, it is like a seed in our heart which will conceives good desires from the heart of our Father.

That is why God passionately loves us. How can He not love His own? By restoring us back to Him, He is restoring that which had been stolen from Him.

The power of God

Romans 1:16

For I am not ashamed of the gospel of Christ: for it is the power
of God unto salvation to everyone that believes...

The Gospel of Christ is the true teaching or revelation of Christ. It is the revelation that activates the power of God to bring salvation to believers. Many people think that salvation is only to do with being born again. After being born again, then what? Salvation means much more than just being saved. It comes from the Greek word 'soteria' which includes deliverance, preservation, healing, health and soundness. Salvation is our ultimate full package of the inheritance we have in Christ Jesus. Jesus gave us so much more than just eternal life. So the revelation of God releases God's power to bring us our inheritance.

2 Peter 1:2-4

Grace and peace be multiplied unto you through the knowledge
of God, and of Jesus our Lord, according as his divine power
hath given unto us all things that pertain unto life and godliness,
through the knowledge of him that hath called us to glory and
virtue: whereby are given unto us exceeding great and precious
promises: that by these ye might be partakers of the divine
nature, having escaped the corruption that is in the world
through lust.

Knowing the promises of God causes His grace and peace to be multiplied in our life. God's power works in us in proportion to the knowledge and understanding we have of it. Through His promises, God has given us all things we need in life. The grace of God working in us increases by revelation. These are things He gave us, irrespective of what we do. We did not do anything to deserve them and we cannot earn them, but they become real to us by knowledge. He has already commanded our supply; His Word is forever settled in heaven. What He has said will remain standing when everything else gets destroyed.

Hebrews 4:12
The word is alive and active...

He used His Word to bring this world into existence. When He said, "Let there be light," the Word knew what to do. It was by His infinite wisdom that the Word knew where to go and what needed shifting and adjusting in order to achieve the purpose it was sent for. When God spoke, He knew exactly what He wanted; He had already conceived it in His mind. He spoke what He had already foreseen. His words carried the creative force to do the exact things He desired.

Man can clearly envisage the type of house he desires. He can mentally picture it and see its form before it is actually built. He then goes on to put the exact details of the house on paper and gives instructions for it to be built. With technology advancing, it is now possible to see the exact image of the house and every single detail, how it would look with certain types of paint, etc., before the foundations are even laid. Once man gives instructions for the home to be built, he expects it to come out as he has seen it in his mind.

That is the faith of God. That is how God created and framed the world, and that is also how we can create things. We are the exact image of God and are formed after His own likeness. We have God's creative power in us. He is the source of all power; the power we have has the same characteristics as God's. Just as, if we go to an ocean and fill a cup with water, the water in the cup will possess the same qualities as the ocean.

It is through His spoken Word that God has supplied exceedingly great promises. It is by knowledge of these promises and believing them to be true that we obtain them. The Word is a faithful servant. It goes on to do exactly as it is commanded. That is the reason why God gave us words and voices. He gave man the ability to create things, to fashion this earth when He gave it to us.

The exceedingly great power

Power is released from the inside to achieve a certain task. No one has ever seen what power looks like, but we see the evidence of its works. Where did this power originate from? We can never comprehend the extent of the greatness of this power. No one knows its limit. We can only get a hint of its magnitude when someone steps out of what we regard as the norm and does what we call impossible.

For us to know that we have the exceedingly great power in us, we need a revelation of it and how to make it work for us. Everything God created is for our good, but if we do not know how to correctly apply it, it is subject to abuse and can be dangerous.

The law of gravity has been set to bring order to physical things on earth. Because of this law, we do not have things flying aimlessly around us and we have control of our movements. We decide the path we want to take and follow it. However, it is the same law which says that if a person jumps or falls from a twenty-storey building, he will break his bones, causing pain and death.

Tongue power

The power we have is to create our world around us, bringing us the things we desire. If, however, this power is used other than for the intended purpose, it can destroy and bring pain and torment to people's lives. An irresistible force is released when we speak faith-filled words; however, speaking fear-filled words also releases a force to create that feared thing. James 3:4 likens the power of the tongue to the rudder of a ship, which sets the entire course of the ship. Your tongue can navigate the direction your entire life will take. In comparison to the ship, it is very small and almost seems irrelevant, yet it overpowers even the mighty winds and aligns to the direction it is set to go. It feels effortless to change the course of life's direction yet incredibly powerful.

Power of belief

There is a powerful force behind every belief. In this world, there are two forces: one of good and one of evil. We are told in James that every good gift and every perfect gift is from above.

James 1:16-17
Do not err, my beloved brethren. Every good gift and every perfect gift is from above, and cometh down from the Father of lights, with whom is no variableness, neither shadow of turning.

The source of power that brings good is only from God. A good tree will bring forth good fruits, and an evil tree will bring evil fruits. God is the Father of lights; there is no darkness in Him and there is no shadow of turning. God does not change; He is the same yesterday, today and forever. All good things are given by God, and so is power for good. All evil things are from the devil. James starts by telling the believers not to be in error or mistaken: "Do not err, my beloved brethren…" Through this scripture, God wants us to be able to differentiate what is from God and what is not.

I heard numerous stories whilst I was growing up about how God can cause evil to come on people. In God, there is no evil. What happens is that we distance ourselves from His love by walking in disobedience; knowingly or unknowingly, we open the way for evil to come upon us. Often it is careless talk that can bring disasters to God's people.

When disasters happen, people cry, asking God why He allowed this-and-that to happen. When we realise our errors and draw near to God, He will draw near to us (James 4:8). He can turn any negative situation into a glorious victory when we draw near to Him. When we ask for forgiveness, He forgives us. God is always waiting for us. By grace He has released His mercies, which Lamentations 3:23 states "are new every morning…" God knows our frame; He does not punish us according to our sins. He is a merciful God. What we must realise is that we have power that is working on our behalf.

We must take responsibility for our choices. With every responsibility comes accountability. Every action we take has consequences. The power is available, and we are using it day in, day out. Most people are releasing the power within them without even realising it and getting results they do not want.

We release power when we believe. In Mark 11:23, Jesus told His disciples they would have what they said when they believed. He illustrated how faith works by cursing a fig tree in the presence of His disciples; the following day, as they passed by that tree, they saw it totally withered from the roots. Jesus demonstrated the power of words when spoken with belief. There is a force that is released through believing.

Jesus also went on to teach them that it is the same with prayer. Every prayer made in faith would produce results. He said:

Mark 11:24
Whatever things you desire, when you pray, believe that you receive it and you shall have them.

Again, Jesus showed us the key: *believe.*

There is one fundamental key to understand which is very important. In verses 25 and 26, Jesus commanded us to forgive people who we have anything against so that God may also forgive us. Unforgiveness hinders the power of God from flowing in one's life. You may meditate daily on the Scriptures and believe that whatever you have asked for is already yours (which is true), you may do everything right, but if you hold any unforgiveness you will see no results. It can hinder your prayers from being answered. Holding unforgiveness is like drinking poison and hoping for someone else to die.

Unforgiveness does harm to the person holding it, whilst the one it is held against goes ahead, enjoying their life. It will put one in bondage and often steals joy and freedom. It is time to let go of the bitterness and grudges you may hold against anyone. Let us release people who have hurt us and start living our lives.

Ignorance can kill

The power we have inside us is so great. No evil can stand it when we exercise our authority. For us to use it we must know that we have it.

Samson knew of the incredible power he had. No one could withstand him until he exposed the secret of his power to the enemy. When his hair was cut off, his enemy came to attack him. So he rose against his enemy just the way he always had, assuming he was going to attack the Philistines as usual. What he did not know was that his strength had already left him. And so he went straight to the enemy, who effortlessly defeated him. They caught him and destroyed his eyesight and gave him a hard life sentence in prison. (Judges 16)

When reflecting on this story, I often think that if Samson had known he no longer had the power he used to have, instead of going straight towards the enemy he might have run away and hid somewhere until his hair had grown and regained his strength. But he assumed he still had the power and was destroyed because of lack of knowledge.

There are things we can confidently go after and do, which are based on our expertise and experiences in life. Often, we just get on and do it without even hesitating. Why? It is because we know the things we are capable of achieving. When we come up against a challenge of something we have never done before, our first reaction may be fear, nervousness and uncertainty – and some will not even attempt the challenge.

Knowledge is powerful. Our faith in God is based on knowledge. Jesus operated in the full knowledge of who He was, why He was here on earth and the power that was within Him. He was not intimidated by the people who opposed Him. He never sought approval from any man because He knew His father's perfect will for Him. He was meek and humble, yet He operated in great power and authority. I believe that is the place we are to operate as believers. Jesus was not afraid to set aside His garments to serve because He was secure in the knowledge of who He was.

We need the revelation knowledge of the Word of God. We need to know who we are and what 'makes' us.

God's power in us is hindered from working by:

- Unforgiveness
- Unbelief and doubt
- Ignorance
- Fear

Release of power

Ever since the creation of man, even though his instant connection with God was lost through the high treason committed by Adam, man still has power within him. Man has gone on to create the marvellous inventions we see today, brought about through his God-given ability and power to create things.

We are told that God's Word is alive and active. Jesus said that the words He spoke were spirit and life. And it is the Spirit that gives life. So this Word, when spoken, goes forth to perform exactly as it is sent to do. It knows how to find its way. The Word of God can reach even the most impossible places, such as dividing the bone from the marrow, and soul and spirit. It is the Word only that is able to discern the thoughts and the intents of the heart. It will penetrate through your mind and emotions and change you. No one can ever tell what is in someone's heart unless God reveals it to them. It is only the Word that is referred to in the Bible that is able to save your soul.

It is through His Word that God has given us good health, prosperity, protection, wisdom, creativity – in fact, everything. This Word possesses the power of God. It comes to us as a seed. If we want corn, we plant corn seed. When we want apples, we plant apple seeds. God's Word has power in itself to bring itself to pass. We do not have to make the Word of God work. All we need is to plant it in our heart and find rest, knowing that it will accomplish its purpose.

Too many times we struggle to make the Word of God work. It is not within our ability; our job is to let God's Word abide in us. We are to abide in Jesus. Jesus was the Word manifested in flesh. Through Him all things were made, and is still the case today. Through Him we can do all things:

Philippians 4:13
I can do all things through Christ which strengthens me.

John 15:5
...without me you can do nothing.

It is through His power and might that we are able to manifest His promises so that they become a reality.

We have got to make that decision. God has given us power to make choices, but often our choices stand in the way, hindering the Word working for us. God's Word is His will for us; if we make choices outside His will, His Word will never work for us. You should not prepare for the worst to happen whilst 'believing' God to deliver you at the same time! You cannot serve two masters at once. The master that you yield to more and make room for is the one who wins.

Fear and faith can never work together. That is why Jesus told Jairus not to fear but to only believe. Jairus went to Jesus and asked Him to come to His house to lay His hands on his daughter. He believed that, by having Jesus lay His hands on her, she would recover. Whilst they were on their way to Jairus' house, someone came and told him not to bother Jesus because it was now too late; the girl had died. Jesus quickly told Jairus not to fear but only believe. (Mark 5:21-23)

Jairus' initial confession was his act of faith. He had spoken what he believed Jesus would do for him. His confession of faith caused Jesus to set out on a journey to go to his house, to fulfil Jairus' confession of faith. If he had said anything else that conflicted with his initial faith-filled words, he would not have seen his miracle. That is the reason why Jesus did not give him a chance to say a word but encouraged him only to believe.

This tells us how the Word of God works. When we speak while believing, the Word goes where it is meant to go. It may take time, just as in the case of Jairus' daughter or that fig tree. Just because we are not seeing instant results it does not mean we should change our confession and confidence in God and start saying the exact opposite to the things we are hoping for. If Jairus believed that Jesus' power could touch his daughter just by Him speaking the Word, he would have asked Jesus to speak the Word only. But he believed that the only way his daughter was going to be healed was to have Jesus lay His hands on her. Jesus ministered deliverance to people based upon what they believed.

The main ingredient here was *belief.* God's power towards Jairus worked for him in accordance with it. I believe his faith came when he heard about the works Jesus was doing in the city. He must have had the revelation that if Jesus was doing all this, "surely He could do it for me". He did not allow his fears and doubts to interfere. He was desperate and determined to get his answer. Some may have hesitated in asking Jesus, assuming, "Jesus wouldn't have time to come to my house. After all, He is a busy man. He wouldn't leave His busy schedule just to come to my house."

This shows how committed Jesus was to anyone who approached Him. It also should reveal to us His commitment to fulfil our desires. As long as we acknowledge His ability and willingness, He can fulfil our deepest needs.

The woman with the issue of blood had also heard about Jesus and she had faith. She confessed that if she could only touch the hem of Jesus' garment she would be healed (the power of enlightened knowledge). Since she was legally not allowed to be around people because of her condition, she only based her faith on what she had heard. She had never seen Jesus doing any acts of healing, but she believed in his healing power. Even though she was weak, she pressed through the crowd until she got to the point of her focus. As soon as she touched the hem of Jesus' garment, healing power flowed through her and she was restored immediately. (Luke 8:43-48)

When you allow His Word to abide in you, He will heal you of the disease for which man says there is no cure; He will deliver you out of any impossible situation; He will raise the dead and He can make you prosper in the midst of recession. He can give you anything that you may ask for. He is the God of the whole earth. It is God in us who does the works.

Jesus said, "...the father in me does the works" (John 14:10). Jesus was saying that He did not speak from Himself. He spoke only His Father's will. His Father's will was expressed in words and demonstrated in power seen through the works. How profound this is!

We need to have sound knowledge of the power of God's Word. We need revelation knowledge to know how great this power is, to obtain revelation of what the Word of God is and what it is capable of achieving. When we learn to release it to perform, the rest will flow. We will find every good thing promised to us. We will discover the true purpose of our calling and become aware of the mighty power that works for us.

God has already provided everything we need before any problem ever existed. All we need is our positive response to what God has already done. God has made everything available for us regardless of our works. It is not what we do that makes God move. Rather, it is our positive response to what He has already provided that makes God's provision manifest to us. Jesus taught His disciples:

Mark 11:24
What things soever ye desire, when ye pray, believe that ye receive them, and ye shall have them.

The secret is in *believing* that we have *received* those things we have asked, before seeing any physical evidence of their existence.

Titus 2:11
For the grace of God that bringeth salvation hath appeared to all men.

God has made salvation available to all men, but not all men are saved. For men to receive salvation, we must believe and take it by faith. It is by faith that we are able to access the grace of God. We cannot make God do things that He has not already made available. He has already moved and made every provision for us through His infinite wisdom. God is waiting for us to use our faith to take what He has already provided.

CHAPTER SIX

Knowledge, Revelation and Wisdom

Joseph was put in prison for an offence he did not commit. Whilst in prison, Pharaoh had a dream which greatly troubled him. Pharaoh knew the details of the dream, but did not understand it as it was not revealed to him. He, however, knew that the dream had a significant meaning. And so he sought for the interpretation of the dream from his wise man and magicians, but no one could give the interpretation. Then Joseph was called to interpret.

- Joseph obtained *knowledge* about the dream when Pharaoh explained it to him.
- Through *revelation* from God, Joseph was able to interpret the dream.
- Joseph obtained *wisdom,* which he gave to Pharaoh in order to plan for the future that Pharaoh's dream was communicating.

The dream would have had no effect had Pharaoh not received the revelation about the dream. Neither would it have benefited him had he not known what to do with it. Application of wisdom will change our lives and enable us to make wise decisions that could save our lives and the lives of our loved ones. With wisdom we will know which path to take in our lives.

God is a God of strategy. All the events that Joseph went through positioned him to be that person who would interpret Pharaoh's dreams. Had he not been there, the Pharaoh would have remained in the dark and would have been caught unaware by severe famine. It meant many nations would have perished. Yet God had revealed its coming while there was still time to do something about it.

God has His ways of communicating with us. He is constantly speaking to His people, but people do not give it much attention because they do not know how significant God's revelation is. If they knew, it would save them from making mistakes and would save people's lives.

CHAPTER SEVEN

The Essence of Knowledge

I remember one particular day in mid-January. It was winter time in England. There had been severe weather warnings issued by the MET Office; it was going to snow 'big time', and they anticipated traffic disturbances on the roads. The advice issued was not to travel unless you really had to. The snow was forecast to start around midday. Even schools urged parents to use their discretion as to whether or not to take their children to school. And so, based on the weather forecast predictions, I decided to keep my children home that Friday.

My husband had a business trip about seventy-five miles away. He went quite early in order to beat the forecasted snow. Everything we did that day was based on the information we had received about the predicted snow. We believed the report we had heard and acted upon that knowledge. The snow had not started yet, but we were confident that the snow would come as predicted. I did my shopping quite early that day and bought enough provisions so that we did not need to travel for a few days.

All these activities were only based around what we had heard. For a moment, I actually asked myself, "What if it doesn't snow the way it is expected?" In my mind, I believed there was no way the snow could fail to fall and, indeed, it snowed as predicted.

Here, I felt the Lord was speaking to my heart: that the kind of faith we demonstrated was the kind of faith that pleased Him. God has spoken Words regarding things He has already given us. He desires us to know the things we have, even though we cannot see them. God said He gave them to us, and so it meant they were there. He just wants us to trust Him. If those things were visible to us, would there be any need for God to tell us of their existence?

We need to have knowledge of who God is and His integrity towards His Word. We need to trust Him completely with our heart, regardless of the situation. He always has a way of making what He promised happen, if we allow Him. He has no limitations or boundaries except for the ones we place on Him. God works through His people. He expresses His love through you and me. Isn't it reasonable for us to think that, if we are to represent Him, He ought to fully equip us with everything we need to make it happen?

We are ambassadors of Christ in the world. We are meant to bring the Kingdom of heaven here on earth and to control every circumstance by the perfect will of God. He depends on our cooperation with Him to fulfil His plans on earth.

We often hear messages regarding the power of believing, such as, "Have faith in God!" "Keep on holding to the Word!" Yet, sometimes we fail to get the things we are hoping for. In our own effort, we try very hard with all our strength to believe; sometimes we think we have the faith but still see no results. Once this fails to get us results, we may decide to fast.

Fasting is a very powerful way of submitting ourselves to getting closer to God. It is preparing our heart to be receptive of the spiritual gifts God has for us. It is a time we spend focusing on God and His Word. This creates an environment of miracles. What we focus on usually gets enlarged, and so our ability to receive from God increases as well. However, fasting does not make God move. It does not make Him do anything He has not already done for us. As a matter of fact, when we are fasting, our spiritual awareness of the things given to us increases as we focus on Him. That brings faith, which makes the things we are hoping for real to us before they even manifest.

So, next time you start fasting, check your motives. Ask yourself, "Why am I fasting? Is it to make me feel that I have done enough so that God will do the things I want?" It is wise to clearly define the purpose of the fast and what you desire to receive from it. Make fasting a time to draw closer to Him. As a result, He will draw closer to you. The closer you get to God, the more magnified He becomes to you and the easier it will be for you to receive His wisdom to create your desires.

It is not our own effort or the length of prayer, it is not how much we say or how much we fast that makes our Christian living practical. It is through revelation knowledge of God that we get to know His purpose for us, His provision to us, and His power that works in us.

Knowledge with understanding

Understanding the knowledge acquired is essential if we are to become effective and fruitful in our knowledge of God. Many regard the Bible as being too difficult to understand. Understanding is like the receiving of seed into the ground where it is sown. It will enable us to grasp the information we receive. Understanding is for our mind. We are able to retain the information we learn when we understand it.

We should realise that everything written in the Bible has a deeper meaning, that we are not capable of understanding the things of God with just our physical mind. Regardless of how learned we are, we can never figure out the things of God without the Holy Spirit. He is the one who gives light to the eyes of our understanding of the Scriptures.

On a personal level, I learnt to recite Psalm 23 when I was eight years old at school. I have known that Scripture most of my life, but it really did not do anything for me until I sought to understand it. I never received any spiritual nourishment from it. I just knew it but never understood what it was really saying.

Anyone can read the Bible and explain what is being said. But the understanding of the message conveyed in it is only understood through enlightenment by the Holy Spirit. He is the One whom Jesus said would lead us into all truth and teach us all things. In Mark chapter 4, Jesus expected His disciples to understand the Parable of the Sower that He taught them. He explained to them that it was the fundamental principle of how the Kingdom of God works. He went on to say that it was given to them to understand the mysteries of the Kingdom.

The parable spoke more about the ground than the seed. It was the same type of seed that fell on different types of grounds. The seed had all its potential in it, but whether it produced or not depended on the type of ground it fell on. It is the seed that produces fruit, not the ground; it is the Word that produces fruit in our life. However, it is the ground that the seed falls on that determines the effectiveness of that seed; if we can receive the Word of God and not get in its way, it will produce a marvellous harvest in our life.

How we receive the Word of God is what determines the effectiveness it has in us. Knowledge is based on information, which is nothing more than the Word. Man's heart is the ground, where we receive the Word. Man is made of the dust of the ground, and the ground is where the seed gets planted. Of the four different kinds of ground, only one type of ground could produce various kinds of harvest.

Understanding is the doorway through which the Word of God enters your heart. If there is no understanding, the devil will quickly snatch the Word away. Understanding is the key to receiving the Word of God in your heart. Knowledge of God comes through the Word of God.

During my high school days, I enjoyed studying History the least. I really do not remember understanding much about what the teachers taught. It was one subject I would have to read over and over again. However, I also had a favourite subject, and I came alive when the Maths teacher walked in.

Another way of getting understanding is by repetition. If you keep hearing the Word of God over and over, there will come a time when you finally get it – just like reading any book or listening to the same music over and over again. There are few movies that I have emotionally engaged in or understood every detail just by watching one time. But there are certain movies I have watched several times, and each time I watch them I always discover, or notice, something new. Have you realised how much easier it is to understand when you read a book more than once? Each time, you understand it better than before. That is what I did with History, and I didn't do too badly in the exams either.

You can know one thing today yet tomorrow totally forget about it. Such knowledge goes as far as the head and that is it. It never goes anywhere beyond our ears and will not produce anything for us.

There is knowledge of spiritual things that is necessary for our spiritual growth, and there is natural knowledge that is required in order to be able to get by. Natural knowledge, such as the rules of the road, does not require divine revelation. Knowledge of how good it is to eat healthily will help maintain our body and keep us full of energy. This is the kind of knowledge we get, for example, when we read Psalm 23, which talks about the Lord being a shepherd. When we read this Scripture, we can see what it is talking about; but it is only when we understand it that it opens the door to revelation. It is then that we begin to be transformed by it and begin to see changes in us.

In all matters regarding things of the spirit, we require the help of the Holy Spirit. That is His mandate to us. I have found that asking Him to reveal what He wants me to understand is one way to start. He will show you deeper things of God from one Scripture that can totally transform your life.

Faith and knowledge

Faith works by knowledge. Philemon 1:6 explains how acknowledging or becoming aware of every good thing which is in us in Christ Jesus makes our faith effective.

We should not struggle to believe. We should not try to convince ourselves that we have faith. Faith will come by hearing the Word of God. It happens when that Word takes root in us. This causes faith to rise.

Knowledge is the pivotal point on which the keys of our destiny hang. Without knowledge, there would be no faith. Before being saved, I heard the message being preached of God's demonstration of His love to us. That He sent His Son Jesus to die for our sins. After knowing about the love of God and the power of salvation, I made a decision to give my life to Him. It was after I had heard about Jesus that faith came and I was born again. Where there is no faith it is impossible to please God. So, what would become of us if we did not have any knowledge?

The knowledge we possess is responsible for making us who we are today. We take action based on what we know. Faith is the language God understands. It is what connects us with God. Being without faith is like a blocked water pipe – water is released from the source, but it never arrives at its destination. Faith is what gives us access to God's grace. Without it, it is impossible to please Him. The Bible tells us that no one has ever seen God at any time, yet we are convinced He exists.

Hebrews 11:6
He that comes to God must believe that He is, and He is a rewarder of them that diligently seek Him.

We have to be filled with the knowledge of what God has provided for us and then we make up our minds to have God's best. The reason why people are not receiving God's best is because they settle for less. If God did not put any limits on what we can achieve, why then are we not aggressively going after it?

For us to get the knowledge to confidently pursue our blessings, we need to be able to understand the nature of our inheritance and how to get it. Jesus said to His disciples:

Matthew 13:14
By hearing ye shall hear, and shall not understand; and seeing ye shall see, and shall not perceive.

What He meant was, they may have heard the truth about the Kingdom of God but they could not understand it because it was not revealed to them. Therefore, it had no effect on their life.

Knowledge of God's principles and ways of doing things, when understood and correctly applied, will make a great difference in releasing God's power to work for us. However, the lack of knowledge of the power of God within us has caused many to become alienated from the privileges in life that God has made available. The things we have been given are under our authority to bring them into the physical realm.

Matthew 9:29
According to your faith, be it unto you.

Therefore, it is never God's fault if we fail to receive the things we desire. God has already done His part. It is our fault when we fail to understand and use what we have been given. He wants us to have full understanding of how powerful we are and the kind of creation we are.

He has a purpose for each and every individual, which He has already mapped out. We are thoroughly equipped with everything as far as this life is concerned. Everyone has an equal chance in life, regardless of the environment we were brought up in or what part of the world we live in. As long as you get to that place of making your own choices and decisions, then what God has placed in you will open the way to its fulfilment. This, however, only happens when you have the revealed knowledge and receive the wisdom to apply it in your daily life.

Heaven is pregnant with gifts God has given to His children. Ignorance is no excuse. When we stand before Him, we are going to be held accountable for what we have done with what we have been given. No matter how big or small our potential, God expects us to use the talents He gave us.

Knowledge of God's will

It is God's will for us to be full of knowledge of His will. If a son does not know the will of his Father, how is he going to please Him? Without full knowledge of His will, it will prove impossible to be confident enough to stick to it when it gets uncomfortable and challenging. You may even hear excuses like, "Well, I guess it wasn't God's will, after all." People who say such things walk right out of God's divine plan for their lives.

Knowing God's will for our life will give us the courage to pursue those things we know are right for us. There will always be resistance, especially when going after the will of God. Unless we put our flesh into subjection it will always fight against the things of God. The flesh can never comprehend them.

> Colossians 1:9
> ...that ye might be filled with the knowledge of his will in all wisdom and spiritual understanding.

Paul prayed the above prayer, desiring for people to be filled with the knowledge of God's will. He was not speaking of head knowledge, whereby we would try to find the logical reasoning behind it in order to get a glimpse of it. He was talking of a much deeper level of knowledge, which surpassed natural understanding. This kind of knowledge is divine and is given by the Spirit of God. This kind of knowledge comes from within, the inside source.

Knowledge is the first essential key element to discovering the path to your destiny, but knowledge alone can never be of benefit to us. In order for enlightenment to come, there must be information to be enlightened upon. Knowledge with understanding to us is like planting a seed. That seed, when it is watered and nurtured, will germinate and grow. We can call that process 'the revelation stage'. It is bringing what is within that seed into realisation. When the plant fully grows and fruit develops, that is what we can call 'the wisdom stage'. This is the level at which we bear fruit, where the benefits of the knowledge acquired and understood now take form.

According to Colossians 1:9-12, the knowledge of the will of God will cause you to develop your faith to:

- Walk worthy of the Lord.
- Be fruitful in every good work.
- Increase in the knowledge of God.
- Be strengthened by His power.
- Be patient and longsuffering.
- Be filled with joy.

Jesus went around doing good works. The Father was glorified through Him because He had knowledge of His perfect will. God is in the process of preparing His Bride and restoring divine order to His Church. He is coming for a Church without spot or wrinkle. He is bringing believers to fulfil divine destiny, which has already been set before the foundations of this world. He has equipped us with everything necessary that we might grow and conform to the image of His son, Jesus. For us to get there, we also need to do our part. We must endeavour to walk in His ways and live a life to fully please Him. Knowledge of His will ushers us onto the right path. God is not pleased when we walk in darkness, where it is impossible to walk worthy of Him and to fully please Him.

Jesus said in John 15:16 that we did not choose Him but He chose us so that we may go and bear fruit that will remain. Fruitfulness is God's will for every individual's life. In order to show how fruitfulness is a serious issue with God, Jesus said concerning every branch in Him that did not bear any fruit that God would take it away (John 15:2).

The danger of ignorance

In the Bible, ignorance is often referred to as living in darkness. It is the absence of light.

1 John 1:5
...God is light, and in him is no darkness at all.

God is called "the Father of lights" (James 1:17), meaning that knowledge, enlightenment and revelation all come from Him. He knows all things and there is nothing that is hidden from Him. Nothing can be concealed in His presence. Everywhere He is there is light because He *is* the light. Darkness can never withstand God's presence.

And so the devil uses the power of darkness to keep people in bondage. He uses those areas we have little or no knowledge of to alienate people from God through deception and lies. He knows that once we receive knowledge of the truth in God, he has no power over us. He knows that the battleground of our warfare is in our mind.

The devil would rather have you and me kept in ignorance than gaining the knowledge of God. The power of darkness operates in areas we are ignorant of. Jesus came to deliver us from the power of darkness:

Colossians 1:13
Who hath delivered us from the power of darkness, and hath translated us into the kingdom of his dear Son.

The "power of darkness" referred to in the above passage is being ignorant of the truth in the knowledge of God. It is where people will find themselves stumbling, making wrong choices and decisions that often lead to destruction. When we receive the truth from the Word of God, we become enlightened:

Psalms 119:130
The entrance of thy words giveth light; it giveth understanding unto the simple.

When the Word of God enters our hearts, it gives light. And from the previous Scripture, we read that God is light. So we see that the light God represents has to do with the knowledge we have of Him.

The devil tries to prevent us from acquiring the knowledge of God. The areas we often see ourselves struggle with in life are areas we are still ignorant about. Ignorance is the weapon he can use to keep us from growing in the knowledge of God. He knows that if we have knowledge, his strategies against mankind will become ineffective. He devises plans to distort the true knowledge of God and makes us question God's integrity in regards to His instructions for our life. Many things that God has said regarding us do not make any sense at all to our physical senses.

Hosea 4:6
My people are destroyed for lack of knowledge.

In an earlier book, I mentioned a story I read about a woman who received an inheritance cheque worth millions of dollars from her wealthy employer. This employer had no family at all and was a very famous and successful artist who sold expensive paintings. The employer became terminally ill and, when she knew that her time to die was near, she gave her illiterate servant this fortune. The servant graciously received it with a grateful heart, took the cheque and placed it in a frame to keep it as a reminder of her employer. She knew it was something valuable as she had a very close relationship with her employer, but she did not know what it was. The only thing she knew was that it had her employer's name signed on it, just as on the paintings she'd sold.

Eventually, this wealthy woman died. The servant had to find another job in order to sustain herself. She continued working hard all of her life and eventually became ill from working so hard. Her son, who lived far away, decided to pay his mother a visit. When he looked around his mother's bedroom, his gaze was caught by a lovely frame that was hung on the wall there. Out of curiosity, he went to take a closer look. When he realised the significance of what was in the picture frame, he asked his mother where she'd got it from. She told her son that she'd been given the cheque years ago from her deceased employer. He explained what the paper was and how millions were lying there waiting for her to make a claim.

What a sad story. Here we have this very wealthy woman who did not know what she was in possession of. All her life she struggled, living in a tiny, worn-out house, yet all the time she was a very wealthy individual. Every night before going to bed, she stared right at her fortune, but her ignorance kept her from enjoying it.

When Abraham Lincoln was still the President of the United States, he signed the Emancipation Proclamation, which freed all American slaves. However, there are documented cases where slave owners hid the Proclamation, and slaves continued serving in bondage because they were ignorant of the change that had taken place.

Imagine – living in bondage all those years because of lack of knowledge! Whatever things you have knowledge of will frame your world. In the world of these slaves, they were still slaves even though the law had freed them from slavery.

The devil uses the same strategy to keep people in bondage. The Bible tells us that we have been redeemed from the curse of the law (Galatians 3:13), but so many of God's people are living a life of constant struggle. The devil will try to keep people in ignorance, and he uses every trick possible to keep it that way. He knows that once you know who you are and how much power you have over him, he will no longer be able to keep you in bondage.

Ignorance kept Gideon, along with the rest of the Israelites, in hiding from the Midianites, whose hand had prevailed against them. In Judges 6:11-14, when the Angel of the Lord appeared to him and said the Lord was with him, Gideon was actually surprised. And so he asked the Angel of the Lord:

> ...but if the Lord is with us, why has all this happened to us? Where are all his wonders that our ancestors told us about when they said, 'Did not the Lord bring us up out of Egypt?' But now the Lord has abandoned us and given us into the hand of Midian.

The Angel of the Lord told Gideon to go in the strength he had to fight against their enemy.

Gideon had knowledge of what the Lord had previously done for his ancestors. He knew that the Lord was their God. But he did not know the power he had or that God's presence was with them. However, due to the oppression that had invaded Israel, the Israelites believed that God had abandoned them. What they believed made them feel hopeless and powerless against their oppressors, hence their decision to hide in mountain clefts, caves and strongholds. It was out of fear and insecurity.

Have you ever been in a situation in which you were almost convinced that God had left you? You would sincerely look at the situation you were in and think, "Surely, if God was here, He would have done something about this."

When the Angel of the Lord spoke to Gideon, He spoke his destiny. Gideon already had the potential within him to defeat the enemy. He needed to know it and believe it in order to achieve it. God did not use the multitude of people in the army; instead, He chose just a few, who demonstrated alertness and awareness of what they were set for. God was proving the point that it was not about their number or their physical build that determined their victory; rather, it was awareness of His power within them that mattered most.

CHAPTER EIGHT

Understanding

Spiritual understanding: the enlightened eye

In 1 Kings 3, the Lord told Solomon to ask for whatever he desired. Solomon asked for an understanding heart so that he would be able to discern good and evil. His request pleased the Lord, and the Lord gave him wisdom and understanding. He also gave him riches and honour.

We cannot separate an understanding heart, wisdom, riches and honour. An understanding heart will always cause us to see things as they really are. Jesus said:

> John 8:32
> *You shall know the truth, and the truth shall make you free.*

The enlightenment of the eyes of understanding is a result of the spirit of truth at work in us. It is seeing a thing the way God sees it. We are told in the Bible that nothing is hidden from God. He knows the end from the beginning. Of course, He does not reveal all things to us, but He reveals the things we are ready to receive.

Manifestation of the sons of God

> John 1:12-13
> *But as many as received him, to them gave He power to become the sons of God, even to them that believe on his name: which were born, not of blood, nor of the will of the flesh, nor of the will of man, but of God.*

77

Receiving is an act of one's will. Every man is given an opportunity to choose the king they yield their life to. It is a decision that every one of us, one way or another, will have to make in a lifetime. God's Kingdom is a spiritual Kingdom and not a natural one. However, by spiritual birth He made us His children and gave us the privilege of becoming His sons. It is our conduct, dignity, relationship with God and our likeness to His character that manifest us to the world as sons. Sons have the power and authority over the affairs of their father. They protect their father's territory and partake of the available inheritance. They establish order in accordance with the father's will. Their lifestyle is mainly based on their father's riches.

When we submit to His ways and rulership over the affairs of our life, we conform to the image of His son (Romans 8:29). This is the Father's ultimate purpose for us. We need to know our legal rights in the household of God and understand who we are.

Submitting to God is always our choice. No one will force anyone to make that choice; it is a matter of the heart. When one makes a choice of receiving Jesus Christ into their heart, they are given the power to become a son of God. The word 'power' comes from a Greek word; this root word also means 'privilege, liberty or right'. So by being born again we have a right and privilege to become the sons of God. God will only work with what you make available to Him. Whatever you choose to seek, that will you find. If you seek understanding of the things of God, you will find it. If you choose to remain where you are, then – guess what? – that is where you will stay.

Galatians chapter 4 explains a very powerful concept about the difference in spiritual levels. Being a child will keep you under the control of this world. A child is not capable of controlling his circumstances; his world is dictated by the parent. A child cannot be left to decide what is good for them. They have no knowledge of the dangers out there.

Being a mother of three children, I understand the different levels of physical growth in children. The type of food you feed to a six-month-old baby is different to that of a five-year-old child. A newborn baby is not capable of eating solid food because his body is not ready for it. The child is kept safe and monitored all the time.

Everything the child does is determined by the parent, together with the type of food the child eats, the choice of clothes to wear, the kind of bed to sleep in, etc. They have no knowledge of why they have to sleep at night, why they have to bathe, why they have to have immunisations, etc. I guarantee that there is no parent who can explain this to their baby and make them understand. Because he is a child, he has absolutely no say in the affairs of his life.

He does not know what kind of family he belongs to, what his rights and privileges are. He just takes what is made available to him. But as the child grows and becomes more mature, he learns things about his life. He learns what is acceptable and what is not in the family. He learns to talk the language of the family and adjust to the family's ways of living. Bit by bit, he learns about the principles of the house. With growth and development, there comes more knowledge and responsibility to make choices. All this is the process of learning until he grows into a man. Subject to him proving himself to be capable, he becomes entrusted with the secrets of the family.

Understanding comes with maturity

This is when the child begins to gain access to what is rightfully his and begins to enjoy it. If he is an heir to the throne, he takes his position and rules.

It is a problem when a child is supposed to grow physically and become more mature but shows little or no signs of progress in development. He gets seen by a specialist to try to determine what could be wrong. Isn't it interesting how quickly people consult a physician as soon as they fail to see any signs of physical progress? Yet how many people are content to stay at the same level, even twenty years after giving their life to Christ? Isn't it wisdom to actually seek what could be wrong if there are no signs of growth in our spiritual walk?

Spiritual matters are more important because they determine the nature and path of our life. They determine whether we rule or are being ruled, whether we are in control or are being controlled. The level of our understanding depends on how much knowledge of God we possess and our maturity:

1 Corinthians 13:11
When I was a child, I spoke as a child; I understood as a child, I thought as a child: but when I became a man, I put away childish things.

There is certain behaviour that can be tolerated coming from a two-year-old child but not from a seven-year-old. God expects us to grow to maturity in the knowledge of Him. That knowledge comes with accountability and possession. If you are spoon-fed, there will come a time to start feeding yourself. If you do not, you are the one who will face the consequences of hunger. There are certain things that can never be revealed to a child, no matter how good they are, no matter how much we love and trust them.

Hebrews 5:13-14 (NIV)
Anyone who lives on milk, being still an infant, is not acquainted with the teaching about righteousness. But solid food is for the mature, who by constant use have trained themselves to distinguish good from evil.

A child is capable of understanding certain things to a certain level. How much can be revealed to the child is based upon how much the child can take. Normally, the student is the one who will determine the pace of the teacher. If the student is slow, he can be given things he is able to handle. If a child is bright, the teachers can give him lessons of a higher level. Our level of understanding determines how much information God can reveal to us. God is already waiting for us to come and get the Kingdom. He will not withhold it from us. He made it easily available to us:

Luke 12:32
Fear not, little flock; for it is your Father's good pleasure to give you the kingdom.

I believe that is why Jesus spoke in parables. It was not to make the Word of God look complicated, but it was to secure the secrets of the Kingdom that would be revealed to those who were ready for it.

Driving a motor car is a good thing. However, it can be dangerous and irresponsible to allow a child to drive without any understanding of road safety rules. Not only could he potentially destroy himself but he could also destroy the lives of innocent people. It is the same with the secrets of God's Kingdom. Without understanding, the principles that are set to bless and increase us may cause more harm than good. I believe that is why Jesus told us to seek first the Kingdom of God.[4] Seeking comes with hunger and determination. There is no other way of searching for God's Kingdom other than through His Word. It is in the process of seeking that we grow spiritually and become mature and ready to receive spiritual meat, when the eyes of our understanding will be enlightened.

It is much easier to make a decision based on an understanding of spiritual things. This grows as we mature in the knowledge of God. The things we often see manifest in the physical originate in the spiritual realm. The Bible tells us that the unseen things created the things we see (Hebrews 11:3). All things seen have their origin from the invisible world. The spiritual realm is where the roots are established. Tackling any issue spiritually is dealing with it right from the roots. We need the light of God to shine in us in order for us to make the right decisions and choices. When we understand how the heavenly concepts operate, it liberates us from operating out of ignorance.

The devil is called "the father of all lies"[5]. If he showed up and appeared to us and told us his plans against humanity and how he works to destroy God's people, I guarantee you that many people would never fall for his plans. It was never God's plan for us to fail. He provided more than enough for us to be failure-proof. As long as we are holding on to His Word, He guarantees to always cause us to triumph in His Name. The Bible says the devil is like a roaring lion (1 Peter 5:8); it does not say he *is* a roaring lion. But the impression the devil want us to have about him is that of a roaring lion.

---

[4] Matthew 6:33
[5] John 8:44

CHAPTER NINE

Revelation

Deuteronomy 29:29

The secret things belong unto the LORD our God: but those things which are revealed belong unto us and to our children for ever, that we may do all the words of this law.

God wants to reveal Himself and His ways to all of us, for us to know and walk in them. He wants us to be aware of what is around us and the things to come. Receiving revelation will enable us to see things that are beyond the natural. This always places us ahead of every game in life, setting us on the right path even though physically it may not appear to be so. It is the Holy Spirit who reveals the secrets of God to us.

We may have attained knowledge through our education; the things of God, however, can only be received from Him alone. Revelation will come by the Holy Spirit through the Word of God in us. He uses the Word to give us revelation. So, for us to obtain the revelation of God, we have to continually feed on the Word of God. We can never separate God from His Word. They are one, and the Holy Spirit reveals things to our spirit.

Revelation will make you see the glory of God in you and have your spiritual sight restored. It has been the mentality of some that not everyone is capable of hearing from God. But it *is* the desire of God to speak to every individual and to reveal things. Where there is no revelation, people will normally live by the doctrine and traditions devised by man.

Daniel 2:22
He revealeth the deep and secret things: he knoweth what is in the darkness, and the light dwelleth with him.

Daniel 2:28
But there is a God in heaven that revealeth secrets, and maketh known to the king Nebuchadnezzar what shall be in the latter days. Thy dream, and the visions of thy head upon thy bed, are these.

God will use His Word to bring revelation into your life. God does not want us to live blindly like the rest of the world. He wants His children to be aware and prepared for the times and seasons ahead. If God showed Pharaoh the things to come through a dream, with its revelation saving many nations, will He not show His plans to His chosen ones?

The spirit of revelation

So far we have looked at how God is the source of godly wisdom, and the Bible says that He gives it generously when we ask. He reveals His wisdom through the spirit of man. Some may call it the heart, others the subconscious mind. It is spirit-to-Spirit connection. Our natural mind cannot comprehend the spiritual things:

Proverbs 20:27
...the spirit of man is the candle of the LORD, searching all the inward parts of the belly.

We need to have knowledge that our born again spirit possesses the very nature of God. We are to be dominated and led by our spirit. This spirit is that which is one with God. It receives the entire download from heaven. We are there to be led and to receive instructions through our spirit.

Naturally, children take on the nature of their natural parents; likewise, true Christians partake of God's spiritual nature. In every believer's life, there is a battle going on. It is a battle for dominance between the inner man and the outer man – our spirit and flesh. The flesh will always challenge the spirit. However, the way to overcome is to keep your mind focused on the truth through meditating on the word of God. Our flesh always lusts after fleshly things.

When we obtain revelation, we begin to see things the way we have never seen them before. Nothing has changed; you just begin to see things as they really are.

Our physical eyes are unable to see spiritual things. The spiritual world created the physical world. Just because we do not see it does not mean it is not there. So if we cannot see the things in the spirit, how are we supposed to know about their existence in order for us to believe it?

1 Corinthians 2:12
Now we have received, not the spirit of the world, but the spirit which is of God; that we might know the things that are freely given to us of God.

We are to know these things through God's Spirit. The Bible says that the Word is our spiritual mirror. It shows us who we are in the Spirit and the things that are ours. We only need revelation to be able to come to full terms with it.

Elisha prayed and asked God to open his servant's eyes when they were surrounded by their enemy. The servant was panicking; he probably thought that he and Elisha were as good as dead. But Elisha was calm; I think he saw how much his servant was troubled and unsettled. God opened his eyes and he saw that heaven's army surrounding them was much mightier than their enemy's army.

Our natural tendency when we are surrounded with trouble is to panic and run about, trying to find solutions to problems which seem impossible to solve. Instead, we should be at peace and pray to ask God to show us what the problem really is. If we could learn to ask God, to see beyond the things we see, we would live peacefully fearing nothing.

The spiritual world is so real. We only require the Spirit of revelation in order to perceive it. Today, you may be facing a seemingly impossible situation; do not be moved by it. Seek to see it as God sees it.

When Jesus was resurrected from the dead, two of his disciples where walking on a journey to Emmaus. They were talking about things that had happened and Jesus came and walked along with them. They could not recognise Him, even though He explained to them what was written in the Scriptures. When they got to Emmaus they invited Jesus to stay. During supper, He took bread, gave thanks, broke the bread and gave it to them. It was at this moment that their eyes were opened and they recognised Him.

His body had been transfigured. From His physical appearance they could not have known Him. But they *could* have known Him had they given attention to the burning in their hearts. Jesus was now in a glorified body and so with their eyes it was impossible to recognise Him. Their spiritual eyes were opened and they saw it was Jesus all along. Even Mary, at the tomb of Jesus, saw Him and thought He was a guard. She actually went and asked Jesus about His body. That is why we need to be spiritually alert all the time. We need to consistently meditate on the Word of God so that we will be able to differentiate between revelation from God and that which is not from God.

We have seen that all the grace God has for us to live by here on earth is already ours in Christ. Now, our need is to have these comprehensive spiritual treasures revealed to us by the Lord Himself:

> **Ephesians 1:18**
> *...the eyes of your understanding being enlightened; that you may know what the hope of His calling.*

In order to draw upon these heavenly provisions, we need the Lord to enlighten our understanding concerning what is ours in Christ Jesus.

> **1 Corinthians 2:9-10**
> *Eye has not seen, nor ear heard, nor have entered into the heart of man the things which God has prepared for those who love Him. But God has revealed them to us through His Spirit.*

As the Holy Spirit uses the Word of God to reveal these matters to us, our faith develops so we might access them by faith. The Scriptures teach us to pray for such spiritual enlightenment.

> **Psalm 119:18**
> *Open my eyes, that I may see wondrous things from Your law.*

In the Word of God, we are told of the wonderful things that God has for His people. If we prayerfully seek the Lord concerning His insight into these blessings, the Lord will enlighten us. His willingness to respond is evident in His word.

Jeremiah 33:3
Call to Me, and I will answer you, and show you great and mighty things, which you do not know.

The Lord delights in giving heavenly spiritual insight to the humble of heart, not to those who trust in their own wisdom and prudence:

Luke 10:21
In that hour Jesus rejoiced in the Spirit and said, 'I thank You, Father, Lord of heaven and earth, that You have hidden these things from the wise and prudent and revealed them to babes.'

This picture of spiritual children humbly trusting in the Heavenly Father to reveal His ways fits perfectly into God's pattern for living by grace. This pattern is humility and faith.

CHAPTER TEN

Wisdom

The spirit of wisdom

Pro 3:13-18
Happy is the man that findeth wisdom, and the man that getteth understanding. For the merchandise of it is better than the merchandise of silver, and the gain thereof than fine gold. She is more precious than rubies: and all the things thou canst desire are not to be compared unto her. Length of days is in her right hand; and in her left hand riches and honour. Her ways are ways of pleasantness, and all her paths are peace. She is a tree of life to them that lay hold upon her: and happy is every one that retaineth her.

Wisdom is the means by which we apply the right principles to get whatever we desire. Wisdom will cause us to make right choices. It will teach us to live a happy life. It will show us how to get wealth. It will give us the right words to speak life-giving words. Wisdom is a force; no one can generate wisdom. It causes people to operate from a higher dimension of understanding and application of acquired knowledge. There are two kinds of wisdom: godly wisdom and worldly wisdom. God is the source of all wisdom that is unsurpassed and infinite. He is the giver of wisdom to all those who ask for it.

The Bible states that wisdom is the principal thing:

Proverbs 4:7
Wisdom is the principal thing; therefore get wisdom: and with all thy getting get understanding.

It should be our ultimate goal in life to get wisdom. The pathway to wisdom begins with knowledge, which is obtained through understanding. Knowledge always comes first, that is why faith comes by *hearing* the Word of God. With knowledge we need the eyes of our understanding to be enlightened in order for us to comprehend. When understanding comes, it is as if a light is switched on in a dark room. Being in a dark room will make you see shadowy images and you can stumble about – there is no confidence or certainty – but when the light shines everything will become clear and you begin to see things as they really are (in the spirit).

Most people have the knowledge of how to use technology without understanding how it works. The problem arises when your computer gets infected with a virus; it totally wipes off your important information, and you have to look for experts to restore it. They not only know and understand how it works but also can make it function as it's meant to. Now that we have things exposed around us, what we require is wisdom. Wisdom will show us how to apply the revealed things to work for us. Knowledge and understanding without wisdom will never benefit us. We need wisdom in order for us to apply the knowledge we acquire.

> **Job 12:13**
> *With Him are wisdom and might; To Him belong counsel and understanding.*

> **Proverbs 2:6**
> *For the LORD gives wisdom; From His mouth [come] knowledge and understanding.*

God is naturally, entirely and invariably wise. In Him is all wisdom in its fullest. Wisdom is the knowhow of doing something. It is the sound application of knowledge. Therefore, wisdom is based on knowledge; however, it goes beyond just knowledge. Many times in Scripture, wisdom goes hand in hand with knowledge. It is the power to see and the inclination to choose the best and highest goal, together with the surest means of attaining it. Wisdom is, in fact, the practical side of moral goodness. As such, it is found in its fullness only in God.

God knows all this. He is the Alpha and Omega. He knows the end from the beginning. Nothing that happens in this world takes

Him by surprise. He is the One who created the world, everything in it and all the people.

He knows what we need before we ask Him. So when we go to Him, let us be mindful that God already saw it coming and He also sees the right way to go. Let us seek God's wisdom in every situation in our life. This wisdom is found within us because God dwells in us. Through wisdom we receive enlightenment to see things beyond the illusion of life and to know what reality is.

Jesus was continually applying the wisdom of God in everything He did. He said, "I only do what I see My Father do."[6] When He came here on earth, He did not come clothed in His glory. He did not come as God to claim back what Adam had lost. He came as a Son of Man, born of a woman. He depended upon the revelation He received from God to do His work. He was God manifest in the flesh.

Jesus was just like any believer. His identity was God, but when He came He was the Son of Man. He was subject to every physical pain and emotion, hunger, feelings, etc. Within Him was the Seed of God, but on His days on earth He was subjected to earthly things. Through divine wisdom He was always in control because He knew who He was. He conquered the devil as the Son of Man and paid for men's wages of sin, which is death as a man.

So, He knew what His journey to the cross would be like. Yet, in the middle of it all, He still applied wisdom to every situation.

Application of wisdom

During the time of Solomon's reign, there arose a dispute between two harlots who lived together in the same house (1 Kings 3:16-28). They had each given birth to sons, three days apart. One of them accidentally slept over her baby and he died. She got up whilst the other woman was sleeping and exchanged her dead son for the living one. The one whose son was exchanged for the dead one brought the matter to the king for judgement. The accused woman denied the allegations. And so there arose an argument. I am sure it was quite a tense situation and difficult to know who to believe. The worst that could happen was that a liar would be rewarded.

---

[6] John 5:19

On hearing the matter, King Solomon simply asked for a sword. As soon as the sword was brought, he ordered that the living baby be divided in two so that each woman would get a half. The real mother, out of love and compassion, cried and asked the king not to harm the baby but to give him to the other woman. But the other woman, who had exchanged her dead son, urged the king to go ahead and divide the child. It was now clear who the boy's real mother was.

That was a wise and understanding heart at work. King Solomon knew that no mother would ever bear seeing her child die. And so he applied wisdom that restored a child to his rightful mother. If King Solomon had had no understanding, he might have made a lifelong mistake in making a judgement over the matter. But through his righteous judgement the whole of Israel feared him because they saw God's wisdom in him.

In 2 Kings 6, Elisha the prophet of God angered the Syrian King when he discovered that Elisha had been responsible for warning the King of Israel about the attack strategies against the country. Elisha would know exactly what the Syrian King was planning against the King of Israel. Every time the Syrian army went to attack the army of Israel, they were waiting for them; the Syrians were defeated every time. The King of Syria was convinced that there must have been a spy in their camp. He was told about the prophet who knew every single plan they made against Israel. So, the king went to attack Elisha. During the night, the army surrounded Elisha and his servant. When the servant got up in the morning, he panicked and told Elisha about them being surrounded. Elisha told him not to fear because they had a greater army surrounding them than what they could see. Elisha also asked God to give his servant eyes to see. And he began to see with his spiritual eyes.

What Elisha wanted to achieve was to have his servant on the same level of faith as him. He wanted him to see what he was seeing in the Spirit. He understood the concepts of faith; fear always contaminates faith and he understood the power of agreement. He knew if the spirit of fear was working in his servant, it would hinder the heavenly army fighting for them. Therefore, he ordered him not to be afraid and told him that there was a much greater army surrounding them than the army he could see. He then prayed to God to open his spiritual eyes to see. And the Lord opened his eyes so that he could see the multitude surrounding them.

Understanding spiritual concepts is so important. God has given us promises in the Bible, but if we do not understand how the principles work to bring those promises to us we may end up saying that the Word of God does not work. An understanding heart is one of the fundamental keys that unlocks your path.

The word 'enlighten' means 'to give the light of knowledge to'. We have physical eyes to see the physical world and everything around us. These eyes are limited only to what they are exposed to. They cannot see beyond what is visible to them. Our physical eyes can only see through the impression of what is presented before them. We are limited to the things we are able to see.

However, we also have eyes that are able to see beyond the natural. These are spiritual eyes, which see beyond the physical and can see things happening thousands of miles away. These are the eyes that can cause us to see the unseen. Our spiritual senses can be trained to be able to see beyond the natural.

We have seen that all the grace resources God has for us to live by here on earth are already ours in Jesus. We now need to have these comprehensive spiritual treasures revealed to us by the Lord Himself.

Knowledge without the revelation and wisdom to apply it is as good as ignorance. To add to our knowledge, the in-depth meaning of the information received must be revealed. When we obtain the revelation, we need wisdom to apply it in order for it to work for us.

Everything provided in the Spirit

In order to gain access to these heavenly provisions, we need our understanding to be enlightened concerning what is ours in Christ Jesus. God has revealed those things He has prepared for us by His Spirit.

1 Corinthians 2:9-10
...Eye hath not seen, nor ear heard, neither have entered into the heart of man, the things which God hath prepared for them that love him. But God hath revealed them unto us by his Spirit...

This means there is no physical way of knowing spiritual things unless by Him alone.

These things have been given to us by grace through faith. Faith is the only way to get hold of them. Grace has provided everything we need to live a good life, but there is only one way to obtain it. I am sure you have read that "faith comes by hearing the Word of God" (Romans 10:17). We need to hear God's Word in order for faith to come, as the Holy Spirit uses the Word of God to reveal to us God's will and provision.

God is spirit; He gives us things in the Spirit. We have to access those things through *our* spirit. The Kingdom of God is not of this world; however, He created us with the ability to relate to the spirit world as well as to the physical world. It is very easy to claim the inheritance your biological father left you because you can physically see and get hold of it. If it was the same with what God had made available to us, there would not be any need for faith. But that is not the case; all things supplied to us are in the Spirit. We get them from the spirit realm and bring them forth into the physical world. The kingdom of this world is limited to the physical elements we see. That is as far as it goes. All the physical things we see are temporal and subject to change. But the unseen things are eternal (2 Corinthians 4:18).

The spirit world is the most powerful world. It is that which brought the physical world into being. There is limitless supply of every provision and power in the Spirit. God gave us access to the spirit realm because we are spirit. Man is a spirit, who has a soul and lives in a body. Our physical body houses our spirit and our soul. The body does not know anything except for the instructions it receives, either from the soul or spirit realm. The soul realm is comprised of the mind, will and emotions. It receives information from the physical realm, through the physical senses and experiences of life. Therefore, our body will naturally respond to whatever information it receives from the soul realm unless the mind gets renewed by the Word of God. The body is physical and so is sensitive to the physical world. It will often drive us to where it feels safe and comfortable.

For us to get the things of the Spirit, we have to put our body under subjection of our spirit. Our spirit should control the body on what to do, how to feel, and how to respond. The flesh is restricted by the laws of this world, but the spirit is not under the law.

Galatians 5:16-17
This I say then, walk in the Spirit, and ye shall not fulfil the lust of the flesh. For the flesh lusteth against the Spirit, and the Spirit against the flesh: and these are contrary the one to the other: so that ye cannot do the things that ye would.

We may not know the exact plan of God for our lives, but our desires should give us clues of the forthcoming things. God always exceeds beyond all we may ask or think, according to the power that works in us. We may be disappointed when our original plans fail, but always remember that God will always have better plans than our own. His plans do not normally go exactly the way we want them to because His ways are always higher than our ways. For man's wisdom is foolishness in God's sight (1 Corinthians 3:19-20), and God's foolishness is wiser than man's wisdom (1 Corinthians 1:25).

Take action!

Our finite minds may not be able to comprehend all that God has done, is doing, or will do in the future, but we know he is going to fulfil his divine purpose here on earth, because he is the Almighty God. From eternity past, God knew what needed to be done here on earth, and so He created *you* specifically to accomplish it. No one else can take your place in the world. However, if you do not use what you have been given, it will be taken away and given to someone else. Take action towards seeking what the will of your Father is. That way, you can rest assured that you are travelling on the right path towards your planned destination.

Epilogue

God's ultimate plan for you

We now understand that God has supplied for everything we need to live a good life as we walk through our life's journey to reach our destiny. Everything provided is waiting for us to receive it. God did not withhold any good things from us; He made them available to all those who will accept them.

God has an ultimate plan for each and every individual who has ever lived here on earth – those living today, those born tomorrow, and even for the unborn children in their mother's wombs. That plan is for all of us to enjoy everlasting life with Him in Glory. God did not create us to be wasted away; He created us the way we are for a purpose. Everything is available for you to receive today. Most importantly He made available salvation for everyone through His son Jesus Christ, whom He made a sacrifice for our sins so that we may live. The decision is yours and the choice is yours. There are many religions, many movements, secret organisations and practices in the world that use the biblical principles to attain wealth, riches and fame. These principles work for anyone who applies them because they are universal laws placed by God to maintain order on earth.

Yes, we can master and apply the laws that govern the universe to acquire worldly wealth, fame and things that give pleasure. It is worth remembering, however, that all our efforts to fulfil the desires of the flesh will ultimately come to nothing. Jesus said:

Mark 8:36
For what shall it profit a man, if he shall gain the whole world, and lose his own soul?

God's plan is for us to reign with Him forever and ever in a perfect world where there is no pain, sorrow, fear or any form of suffering. You might be thinking, "How can I qualify to dwell with the Lord?" The answer is, you will never be able to qualify on your own merit or through good deeds. It is just not possible. But Jesus Christ qualifies us. He is the Lamb of God that took away the sins of the world. He paid the wages of our sins which was death (Romans 6:23). He died in our place so that we can live.

What next?

It is never too late to surrender your life to Him. Regardless of what you may have done, the price for your sins has already been paid when Jesus was crucified on the cross of Calvary. It is already done; He is waiting for you to choose to give your life to Him.

Jesus is the saviour of this world. He is the only one who has the power to take away our sins and give us eternal life.

> **John 3:16-17**
> *For God so loved the world, that he gave his only begotten Son, that whosoever believeth in him should not perish, but have everlasting life. For God sent not his Son into the world to condemn the world; but that the world through him might be saved.*

Salvation is in Jesus Christ alone. Make the decision today to receive the eternal life He made available to everyone. Salvation is here right this moment. Receive it now! God sees all and knows every heart. Open your heart to Him right now; let Him come in. Give God a chance to show you how good He is!

> **Psalms 34:8**
> *O taste and see that the LORD is good: blessed is the man that trusteth in him.*

If you would like to receive this gift of eternal life then invite Jesus into your life; ask Him to forgive all your sins and make Him your Lord and saviour. Jesus is already standing and knocking on the door of your heart (Revelation 3:20). Open it up for Him and let Him come in! Feel free to speak with Him the way you feel best, or you may like to pray like the following prayer:

> *Heavenly Father, I come to you in the name of Jesus Christ. I thank you for sending your son, Jesus, to die for my sins. Forgive me for all my sins. I acknowledge them along with my shortcomings and my need for a saviour. I acknowledge that Jesus Christ is the son of God, who lived and died and rose again for my redemption. I receive Him now as my Lord and saviour.*

Come in now, Jesus; be my Lord and be my guide. I declare that I am now born again! Thank you for saving me! Amen.

Contact the Author

To contact the author, please send an email to:

tracey@traceymuponda.com

More information about the author can be found online:

www.traceymuponda.com

Related Books by the Publisher

Alive for a Purpose
Amoateng Kofi Owusu

The purpose of this book is to serve as a catalyst for you to be inspired to discover *your* purpose, re-discover your purpose and to take what you have to the next level. The author takes you through over seventy (70) Biblical Basic Keys and Principles to think and act on purpose. This book will change your thinking into believing that you are alive for a purpose and that living and fulfilling God's idea for your life makes life worth living.

Calling Things that Are Not as though They Were
Barb Witt

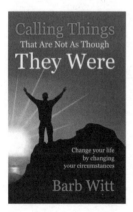

One of the most misunderstood concepts of faith in the Bible is found in Romans 4:17: "God, who quickeneth the dead, and calleth those things which be not as though they were." Barb Witt takes us on a journey through the scriptures, showing that this principle is at the heart of many of the greatest moments in Israel's history, as well as being an important key to Jesus' ministry. This same principle is still active today and is vital to manifest the promises of God in our lives.

Books available from **www.onwardsandupwards.org**